Be Not Afraid of My Body

A Lyrical Memoir

Darius Stewart

Belt Publishing

T0035066

Copyright © 2024 by Darius Stewart
All rights reserved. This book or any portion thereof may not be
reproduced or used in any manner whatsoever without the express
written permission of the publisher except for the use of
brief quotations in a book review.

Excerpts from Essex Hemphill copyright © 1992 Essex Hemphill
from *Ceremonies*, reprinted by permission of
the Frances Goldin Literary Agency.

Printed in the United States of America
First edition 2024
1 2 3 4 5 6 7 8 9

ISBN: 978-1-953368-90-4

Belt Publishing
13443 Detroit Avenue, Lakewood, OH 44107
www.beltpublishing.com

Cover art by David Wilson
Book design by Jordan Koluch

More Praise for Darius Stewart's *Be Not Afraid of My Body*

"This book is a mammoth creation and is actually a literal moving monument to fear and lovely obsession with our bodies' memories. Just unbelievably rich art right here."

—Kiese Laymon, author of *Heavy: An American Memoir* and *Long Division*

"Calling *Be Not Afraid of My Body* artful belies just how readable, dazzlingly propulsive this book is. I already can't wait to read it again."

—Kaveh Akbar, author of *Calling a Wolf a Wolf*

"In lyric prose and fearless voice, Stewart brilliantly confronts, defies, celebrates, and pays homage to our human limitations and limitlessness."

—Susan Steinberg, author of *Machine*

"A memorable portrait of Black gay life, from poverty and adversity to accomplishment and poetry."

—*Kirkus Reviews*

"I read this book in one breathless sitting, often heart-choked and always enrapt."

—Sarah Viren, author of *To Name the Bigger Lie*

"Reading the marvelous (it is indeed a marvel!) *Be Not Afraid of My Body* incited a very particular need in me: to lovingly strike Darius Stewart because what else is there to do when his just-don't-make-no-damn-sense brilliance leaves you ecstatically bewildered? It is a common practice in Black churches: the need to lovingly strike because, say, a member of the choir's voice has inched you closer to the divine. Within these pages is another voice, a literary one, that inches us ever closer to the divine."

—DK Nnuro, author of *What Napoleon Could Not Do*

"*Be Not Afraid of My Body* is a gift, an assembly of grace, wit, candor, outrage, bewilderment, charm, and wisdom of stunning beauty."

—John D'Agata, author of *Halls of Fame: Essays*

"A heart-wrenching exploration of sexuality—how it's discovered, how it's exploited, how it blossoms. Stewart's is a voice we've been waiting for."

—Sarah Blake, author of *Clean Air*

"Darius Stewart's *Be Not Afraid of My Body* is a memoir of haunting beauty that captures, in language bone-clean and sure, the complexities of being Black, gay, and southern in America. Never have I met on the page such steadfast tenderness, such grace for one's past transgressions, such beauty in the face of heartache and grief."

—Alonzo Vereen, author of *Historically Black: American Icons Who Attended HBCUs*

FOR FRY

He stands
like Rapunzel,
waiting on his balcony
to be rescued
from the fire-breathing
dragons of loneliness.

. . .

He stands
like Rapunzel,
growing deaf,
waiting
for a call.

—Essex Hemphill
"Song for Rapunzel"

Table of Contents

Part I: Etymologies

Part II: Nobody Has to Know

Part III: Some of Us Are Genetically Predisposed

Part IV: Patient Zero

Part V: Code Blue Theater

Part VI: You Don't Have to Like It

Part I

ETYMOLOGIES

Through some other
set of eyes
I have to see you,
homeboy,
fantasy charmer,
object of my desire,
my scorn,
abuser of my affections,
curse, beauty,
tough/soft young men,
masked men,
sweet swaggering
buffalo soldiers.

—Essex Hemphill
"The Tomb of Sorrow"

Get Ghost

magine you are a young blackboy in Knoxville, Tennessee—
say, fourteen years old—who doesn't know what a stalker
looks like until a fat, old whiteman with rosacea and gray-
white hair spies on you from his tan sedan.

You've been warned of these whitemen, also known as
the neighborhood spooks, and to beware.

He might have a friendly name like George and the
temperament of someone grieving his youth, which meant
everything to him, and he may want to get it back however
he can.

He wants consolation prizes, and he's open to the idea
of young blackboys, although he usually prefers a particular
one. This young blackboy might be the one who comes into
his corner store to buy soap or floor wax for his mama.

This whiteman likes to think he's reaped a bounty when
he watches this young blackboy with other young blackboys.

Does he imagine he might one day play daddy to the whole brood? Or in his heart, is it only this young blackboy whom he desires because it is only this young blackboy whom he hopes will succumb, eventually, to his longing?

In the early evening, when he closes his store, he might imagine letting this young blackboy fuck him in the ass behind the deli counter, where the two of them will be out of view on a pallet of newspapers and plastic bags.

He might imagine this young blackboy at night, clicking off the lights to sleep the way a child does in his mama's home—she in her bedroom at the front of the house, his brother in the bunk above him, his sister in her bedroom across the hall—the family secured behind locked doors and latched windows (but only some of them safe).

And waiting for tomorrow, in the hours between closing time and those imagined fuck sessions, he might sit alone in his most comfortable chair in a bathrobe, lurking in the light of a floor lamp, lifting a cup of cold brown tea from its saucer, slurping it down while his other hand pulls aside the curtains to peer into the dark night, impatient for morning.

Without this young blackboy, who in the whiteman's orbit is an entire constellation, he might fall into despair, as if the infinite stars in the sky had vanished forever. He might no longer have an opportunity to reduce the blackboy to basic parts: two eyes, a mouth and jaw, nose, torso, legs and thighs, a blackboy's feet.

These are not just parts, but parts the whiteman is determined he can do anything to.

———

You never knew you'd become someone desirable.

You vaguely notice the whiteman's car—that wherever you go, so does he.

He always drives the roads that form the route from your granddaddy's house to yours. You aren't supposed to go to your granddaddy's house after school; you are to go straight home. But you want to watch *The Rockford Files* and *The Andy Griffith Show* with him, and then you'll leave for the twenty-minute walk to East Fifth Avenue.

Over hilly South Olive Street, so close to home, you sometimes get tired, so you sit on the steps of the Korean church with its dark red, almost magenta brick portico, stained-glass windows, and high steeple.

One day, you linger too long because you don't see him parked at the curb.

Like a ride? he says.

No, thank you, you reply.

And he drives away.

You start home again, and when you reach the bottom of the hill to stand at the corner of South Olive and Magnolia, waiting for the light to change, there he is again, heading east on Magnolia toward you.

How did he get there so quickly?

Your family has only recently moved into a house on East Fifth, so you aren't aware of any shortcuts, especially any he might've taken.

He stops at the light, forcing you to cross in front of his car.

Like a ride? he says.

You say nothing.

A fire station across the street becomes a potential haven if necessary.

Whatever routes you think you can take to get home, it doesn't matter. He is there.

So you seek safety elsewhere, the convenience store where you used to steal bubble gum when you were in middle school. On those days when he appears, you flee inside and wait him out, remaining there while you roam the aisles of candy bars, warm two-liter soda pop bottles, and motor oil until you're certain enough time has passed, certain he's gone. But he won't be.

Eventually, you sprint home in short bursts, hiding behind strangers' houses to rest, to catch your breath before continuing.

He finds you anyway.

His persistence is what frightens you most, as if he really can do anything.

You can't outsmart him, can't outpace him, but you need to try.

So you run, and you run faster, and when he's there—*Like a ride?*—you run even faster.

You cut corners through yards. Slip through openings in the neighborhood's maze of alleys and fences his car can't get through.

You run without looking back. Like you've stolen something.

You dart across the lanes of Magnolia Avenue traffic.

You pray you catch the light.

You head toward RT Clapp, the auto repair shop; it's always frantic with people. And once there, you are so close to home. You tear across the parking lot that abuts the edge of your backyard, where you once poured a trail of gasoline from a red can used to fill the lawn mower and then lit it, watching it blaze until it gave up too much smoke. You run, petrified, like you did that day.

You run as you always have from him, a fat, old whiteman in a tan sedan who, sixteen years later, when you are thirty—*Like a ride?*—creeps up on you again as you wait on Magnolia Avenue to catch a bus. Only now he's driving a silver Mercedes. He is the same fat, old whiteman who intends to make you his boy, and all of your thirty years turns away running, forgetting about the bus and where it is you're supposed to be, racing home to your mama's house on Woodbine, praying you leave no trace for him to sniff you out ever again, praying to be swifter, that the engines and pistons of your arms and legs won't ever shut down, praying for breath to fill your lungs, your chest expanding so you can run, run, run like a young blackboy just trying to get ghost, praying that fat, old whitemen will forever just go away.

Picaresque

Before a fat, old whiteman chased me to my house on East Fifth Avenue, I lived in an apartment in the Lonsdale Projects, where, as a bony eleven-year-old blackboy, I came of age when I began to express something akin to love by kissing my pillows. Except I didn't imagine my pillows were other girls or those women with bodies like *Solid Gold* dancers in the posters my best friend, Maurice, kept hidden away in his bedroom; these women wore slinky dresses in a variety of primary colors, and all of them had bodices bunched around their waists to reveal naked titties with erect nipples, their skirts pulled to the tops of their thighs, cocking enough leg to send any other boy but me into a frenzy.

My pillows, I imagined, were any one of the blackboys I watched night after night, their shirts off, playing basketball down the street inside a chain-link fence, sweat beads glistening on their skin like rhinestones mined from a cave deep within our ghetto. They'd dunk and hang, gripping the netless rims, bodies swaying until they released themselves to do it again, up and down the court, the sound of dribbling filling the air with a metallic ring, their sneakered feet light on the concrete as their bodies spun in and out of fake reverses and crossovers, breathing heavy as the ball passed between their legs or behind their backs, drawing contact, slick skin smacking against slick skin.

Each night I returned home to sink my head into one of my pillows, dreaming of those sweat-grimed blackboys scaling the fence when the ball game was over, all of them off in different directions with their shirts draped over a shoulder and their jeans slung low, barely containing their round, firm asses, giving them the appearance of waddling rather than running in the darkening dusk, the hour when their mamas would appear on porches to call their boys home.

I like to think my adolescence was like this: a mostly charming, sweet coming of age, even before I first knew I was a blackboy in love with other blackboys, acting on those feelings by pretending my pillow was a blackboy, pressing my head into its plush belly and sleeping until I woke the next morning with that pillow steeped in drool. My lover-boy pillow was my comfort. Anyone—if ever I dared to let them—could see the intimacy we shared, coupling as we did, the way I surrendered so easily to the pillow's soft girth on those mornings when the light drew across both of our faces a candid moment of repose.

But my adolescence wasn't like this.

Just as I watched those blackboys scale the fence enclosing the basketball court, so did I witness the iron gates erected like prison bars around the neighborhood, gates meant to narrow escape routes, to cut blackboys off at the pass so cops could chase them down into chokeholds. I'd seen them writhe beneath a policeman's grip like they'd done a thousand times before, when wrestling themselves away from one another with trick moves they'd invented or modified from techniques they'd seen on *WWF Superstars*—almost like a rite of passage in case, one day, they'd have to protect themselves in police custody, juvenile hall, or prison. Those blackboys were always safest in my fantasies—plush cushions I kept protected in my arms.

————

As an eleven-year-old boy aware of his same-sex attraction to the blackboys in the neighborhood, I didn't find anything particularly wrong with these desires. After all, I was following a natural inclination, oblivious to the way the world saw me.

That is, I was until Daddy caught me prancing around my bedroom wearing my sister's fluffy, pink slippers, pretending to be queen of my own parade.

He stood in the doorjamb with smoke coiling around his eyes because I was that hot. Or else he refused to believe his own son could be a faggot. He did nothing at all except to harden his face, as if he intended his silence to trap me in the shame of what he'd caught me doing. It worked, and I couldn't help but feel as if I'd been reduced to a thousand winged insects imprisoned in a jar with no route to escape.

Perhaps, too, Maurice peeped my peculiar mannerisms—my penchant for Hula-Hooping with the girls during recess, for jump rope and hopscotch, for exclaiming to him every chance I could about how beautiful his penmanship was. So perhaps it was no coincidence that Maurice stopped by to see me the day Daddy caught me for the second time marching around in my sister's slippers because he believed my behavior was pathological, which is why he crept again up those stairs and cocked his ear to the shuffling noise my feet made against the floor, and, *nuh uh*, he may have thought, *no son of mine*, when he assumed that something wasn't quite right with his eldest boy, who didn't know enough to close the door so he wouldn't be so easily frightened when his daddy appeared suddenly through the smoke that rose once more from those eyes set in a face hard as condemnation, meting out its unbearable punishment: silence.

That day, Maurice hadn't come to save me, however. We set out to walk a few blocks until we found the bench at the bus stop around the corner from my apartment. This was intentional, and Maurice wasted no time launching into a story of sticking two fingers in a girl's vagina because he couldn't help but to remind the other preteen boys that he was the first of us—if not the only one—to fuck a girl. While he talked, he held me in his gaze, and I became a specter of a once-present thing, as if I were only there to fall prey to my own self-consciousness.

Have you even seen pussy before? he asked me.

Yes, I said, meaning only in the pictures from all those discarded copies of *Dark Skin Honeys*, *Players*, or *Bold Black Babes* I'd found around the dumpsters where the single moms and their come-and-go boyfriends lived, in alleyways, and sometimes along the creek bed by our elementary school.

What it look like? he said. How many holes a pussy got?

And like that, I was caught pretending, and I failed. I had no way to escape this truth, nor to tell it—for I had no interest in penetrating the female anatomy then, nor had I any intention of growing into it, but on the contrary, I was destined for a range of options with men. And though I sat right there next to Maurice, trying to contrive an answer, I did so in a body already evolving decades into the future, when a bench could be at a bus stop but also in a park at night, where only in a certain light could a pair of lips move like a ventriloquist's, inviting me to touch, to kneel down not in prayer but for the promise of another man's body.

Come on, let's go, he said. He knew I couldn't answer his questions. And why.

And, he added, quit all that fucking Hula-Hoopin' and shit.

And then he walked me home, which seemed countries away from where we'd been. We said nothing to each other, and every few paces he would look over at me but only briefly, as if there was still something more about me he needed to discover. But without venturing, he simply continued walking ahead.

Thereafter, I began to experience those woeful *pray-the-gay-away* nightly rituals that had me hunched beneath the covers in the darkest dark, anxious and pleading that what my daddy and Maurice knew about me would only be short-lived.

Some nights, I'd hear a voice like a preacher's but not exactly. Perhaps it was that of the man who often stood downtown on the corner of Gay Street and Summit Avenue, disheveled in a two-piece suit, holding a flimsy cardboard placard with a Bible verse written on it as he hollered at passersby: *When a boy's drowning, it's best he doesn't frighten easily or fight the hands tugging him deeper into the eddy. Let the limbs go slack as the water embraces his body, as he is submitting to the will of the Lord. Let the river make him part of it . . . drowning is, after all, an existence. Whether during his life or after, the dead will, for good or ill, be an example for the lives of others. And remember . . . fire doesn't burn what it consumes, it vanquishes it.*

I'm sure I got some of it wrong, what the voice actually said, but whatever he'd said was about death. And as a child, I didn't want to believe in dying. I wanted to grow up expecting failure in between the successes and the further failures to come, and I was fine with that.

But then, as if some manifestation of the voice's message, there were those nights when I dreamed of trekking alone until I reached the edge of a lake, far away from home, where I rolled my pants to my knees to wade into shallow water. My naked feet—calloused and walk-weary—would slide across pebbles, feeling the small tides ebbing to shore and washing over my skin, up to my ankles. I would gaze out at the lake's expanse, at the image of two blackboys huddled cheek to cheek, hip to hip, their arms grazing, hands entwined, walking together. They would throw back their heads in laughter, but in this dream, there would be no sound, only the image of rippling water.

I would stare as a curtain of blackbirds descended upon them, swooping and fluttering until the blackboys parted, revealing them as nothing more than gauze, filaments of dark cloud rolling at the silver rim.

Then their limbs would reassemble, muscular entanglements, like knots of vine latticing trees, and a fist would appear through the arced moon, an ornament gliding down an arm that had also begun to form. Their bodies, fully whole again, would appear undulant on the lake's surface, and together, they would splash into stars, swim stroke by stroke through chilling membrane, determined to wade, ecstatic, in the nook of the moon.

Always before I woke in the morning, the scenery would change, and the surface of the lake would become a dark street on which the two blackboys were walking, their silent laughter continuing, and then, one by one, houses would appear on either side of the road. The sounds that I could not hear that the two blackboys made echoed in the street, eased under doors, and tapped against windows, raising bodies formerly tucked away in bed. Newly opened eyes searched for what had wrestled them from their dreams as they fumbled in darkness, bracing themselves on bedposts, hands pulling back curtains or twisting open the blinds, their red-rimmed eyes squinting into the night, focusing until at last they could see in the street two pairs of arms wrapped around one another, two heads tilted and drawing closer, lips lingering, caressing, tongues flitting in and out . . .

The hiss of sucking teeth could not be heard, nor could the cracking of knuckles as the hands inside the houses gripped the curtain seams tighter. But the windows would begin to glow as if enflamed, then a single lick of fire would return the blackboys to the surface of the lake. And at the bank's edge, I didn't witness drowning. I watched them burn.

Etymologies

The universal principle of etymology in all
languages: words are carried over from bodies
and from the properties of bodies to express the
things of the mind and spirit. The order of ideas
must follow the order of things.

—Giambattista Vico

On the morning of the Lonsdale Elementary School
fifth-grade spelling bee, only three of us remained—
Maurice Jackson, Celeste Whiteside, and me—and
my word was *essential*, from the late Latin *essentiālis*, meaning:
absolutely important, extremely necessary. As in: we were in a
corridor near the school's front entrance, lined against a glass
wall that separated the cafeteria from the main office, and I
turned to glare at Maurice, who was sitting against the wall,

tapping both of his feet, as if to tell me it was *essential* that I hurry the fuck up.

The official rules allowed me two minutes and thirty seconds to spell my word, but Mrs. Wolfe hadn't used a timer all morning, even at the start of the competition, when there were ten or so of us. She'd given us what she believed was an appropriate amount of time, and I wasn't about to let Maurice rush me now.

Eyes forward, Mrs. Wolfe said.

Maurice and I had been friendly since kindergarten because we were always in the same homeroom. But we had only recently become best friends when we caught each other one day after school, walking on opposite sides of a creek bed, tossing our homework into the shallow water. We watched as the only D I'd ever earned drifted alongside yet another one of his Fs.

Nigga, all these years I thought you was smart! he said.

I didn't say "nigga" back then, so I said, Fool, I *am* smart! and began to cross the six-feet-wide creek using the large stones that jutted through the shallow, eddying water. When I'd made it halfway across, I saw in my periphery the flash of Maurice's body leaping through the air. Like I'd seen many of the other boys do before, and which I could not ever summon the courage to do myself, Maurice had taken a running start to clear the six-foot gap. He landed low to the ground, with one knee bent level with his front foot, his hands placed shoulder-width apart in front of him, and I knew this stance immediately: the crouch start position. Maurice wanted a race, so I quickened my pace, trying to maintain a steady balance, but I couldn't, and I slipped on one of the stones and into the water. Submerged to just above my ankles, I felt the cold water filling my shoes as I staggered out of the creek bed. Maurice was now jogging in place as he waited for me to make it to the bank before he sprinted away. I ran after him, hating the feel and sound of my sopping wet socks squishing inside my shoes, yelling for him to slow down, wait up.

Maurice and I went on to Northwest Middle School the next year, and though we only had math together, our status as one another's ace boon coon was never more solidified than when I accidentally impaled him with a freshly sharpened pencil. I'd tossed it to him to hold for me so that I could fight a blackboy we called Skillet, who'd been bullying me all class long. When the fight was over, I looked around for Maurice for his approval, essentially to know if he'd seen how I didn't let Skillet get a lick in, which is how I imagined Maurice would put it when he told his version of events to all of our friends and anyone else eager to hear the details of how *Darius beat the shit out of that nigga*. I made my way through the dispersing crowd, and the first thing I noticed was the pencil protruding from Maurice's forearm.

I'm aight, he said, I'm just glad you beat his ass.

But I began to question just how close we really were when halfway into our sixth-grade year, my family and I moved out of the apartment in the projects and into our house across town on East Fifth Avenue. Maurice and I spent less and less time together when school ended. By the end of summer break, we didn't see each other at all. To my surprise, he eventually moved to the east side two years later, when we were in the eighth grade, but he lived nowhere near where I lived, which is why I went to one school and he to another. It wouldn't be until high school that we'd see each other with some regularity, but instead of celebrating a revival of our friendship, we each settled in with our new comrades, accepting that we belonged to totally different circles.

––––––––

Contretemps. From the French *contre-temps*, against time, meaning: an inopportune occurrence; an untoward accident; an unexpected mishap or hitch. As in: at the end of our senior year, some of us received our college acceptances and some were content simply to mark the end of an era with a high school diploma and forever bid adieu to what had been a protracted *contretemps* for most of their lives. Maurice did neither and instead, as a last hurrah, spent a night drinking with three of his friends, riding shotgun around town.

He insisted on playing the DJ, getting everybody crunk, bumping the music too loud while the driver made sharp turns, eventually crossing the center line as he sped around the curve of Martin Luther King Jr. Avenue into the path of an oncoming car that didn't have its headlights on. There was no time to hear the horn blaring until it was too late, and the car carrying Maurice and his friends swerved into a streetlamp. Three of them suffered serious injuries. Maurice was ejected through the windshield onto the grass, his already dying body landing just outside the streetlight's shining cone.

Essential, Mrs. Wolfe said. You have thirty seconds.

———

Celeste showed more patience than Maurice. I turned to her, hoping she might calm my nerves, but she leaned against the wall with her head bowed, preventing me from seeing her face. She had long lashes and the roundest, brownest eyes, but she kept them veiled by gazing at what might have been a speck on the floor. She gave me a slight smile, as if to tell me she knew of my attempt to solicit her attention, then let her mouth retreat back into its coy pout.

———

Promulgate. From the classical Latin *prōmulgātus*, meaning: to make known openly or publicly. As in: it was essential to the schoolyard blackboys to know whether I liked boys or girls, and so they used urban legends to trick me into believing that they had the power to *promulgate* my sexuality on a playground by the way I reacted to their taunts. These blackboys would take turns convincing the rest of us—but especially me—that if my hand was larger than my face, then I was a faggot; or that if hair grew on my knuckles, then I was a faggot; or that if my middle finger was longer than my other ones, then I was a faggot. They'd single out a few boys to prove they were not, but I was the only one they turned to, demanding, circling.

Let's see your hand, Darius, they said, waiting.

————

Avail. From the Latin *valēre*, meaning: to have force or efficacy for the accomplishment of a purpose; to be effectual, serviceable, or of use. As in: On the day I first noticed Celeste, I stood in the lunch line goofing off with Maurice when she took her place at the end of it, and I knew then that I must *avail* myself of a plan to make her notice me too. If I were older, I might have said she was *beautiful*, but at nine, *pretty* was the highest superlative I knew.

Celeste lived with her grandmother across the street and a few apartments down from my family on Minnesota Avenue. I would visit her there, though she was only allowed to talk to me on the front porch through their screen door. Her grandmother had strict rules about her talking to boys—even one who was nine years old—and especially about what Celeste was allowed to discuss. Most importantly, she was never to mention why she had moved so suddenly from her home in Virginia without her mama and daddy.

Perhaps because of these visits, a rumor started that Celeste and I were boyfriend and girlfriend—the fact of the matter, even at our age, was that we couldn't fathom boys and girls being just friends. But I saw these rumors as an opportunity. Celeste would be my problem solver if I could convince the blackboys on the playground that if we weren't boyfriend and girlfriend—which she insisted we weren't—I at least had a crush on her.

After elementary school, just as it had been with Maurice, when Celeste and I lost touch, she became essential to the terrible lies I told to hide my sexuality, and even—and probably worse—when I was out but still shamed by the stigma of being gay. Among the worst lies I told to folks was that when Celeste and I were teenagers, I'd impregnated her not once but twice. But she miscarried each time.

She and I reconnected briefly in our late twenties while riding the late-night Magnolia Avenue bus: me on my way home from bartending and she from her job as a certified nurse's assistant. As we rattled down Gay Street to Summit Hill and Broadway, turning toward her neighborhood of potholes and teenagers who, during the day, played chicken on their bikes in the middle of the road, she complained to me about the minimum-wage paychecks that were too small to buy a new alternator for her car or to keep up with the rent on her duplex. She was a single mother and showed me pictures of her children on her phone; that night, they were at her next-door neighbors' and, oh, how they got on Celeste's ever-loving nerves. But her eyes grew dark, as though a gloaming occluded her vision, as she looked upon and touched her children's faces on the screen, as if her only regret was that she too often didn't have the chance to feed and bathe them, that someone else would have already whisked them off to bed before she'd gotten home from working all day. I did my best to forget that many people—nearly all of them people Celeste didn't know—believed she had no children, that none were even possible, that not even a miracle from God would grace her with any because my lies about her had made this an impossibility. So as we caught up, I could only hide my shame behind a grimace, feeling *penitent*, meaning: I imagined the

love she had for her children might one day translate into
absolution for me.

———

Essential, I said.

I paused briefly to mouth the letters one more time before
I spelled. E-S-S-E-N-T-U-L-E. Essentule. I turned to Celeste,
who'd lifted her eyes from the floor, a shy smile forming
on her face the way I'd seen it often when she spoke softly
through her grandmother's screen door. And I returned it,
the same bucktoothed grin as when I first noticed her take
her place at the end of a very long lunch line when we were
in the third grade. And so it only made sense that she was the
one I rooted for when I heard Mrs. Wolfe say, Sorry, but that
is incorrect.

———

Immigrant. From the Latin *immigrānt-em*, meaning: one
who or that which immigrates; a person who migrates into a
country as a settler. As in: not to be confused with *emigrant*,
from the Latin *ēmigrānt-em*, meaning: one who removes
from his own land to settle (permanently) in another; as in:
I won my first essay contest imagining how an *immigrant*
might enjoy visiting the Sunsphere in World's Fair Park,

attending the Ringling Bros. and Barnum & Bailey Circus at the Knoxville Civic Coliseum, or cheering on the University of Tennessee Lady Vols basketball team at Thompson-Boling Arena.

———

Three years after losing the fifth-grade spelling bee, I redeemed myself at Whittle Springs Middle School. The students from Section 8A and 8B who scored the highest on the weekly spelling tests in language arts were invited to participate in a competition. I had *the* highest score, having averaged 125 out of a possible 125—which meant I also correctly spelled the more difficult bonus words on every test.

Once again, I made it into the top three, and eventually, I was the only contestant left. If I correctly spelled one more word, I'd be the winner. Mrs. Hanks pronounced *immigrant/emigrant*, and I panicked. I knew there were two ways to spell it, and I wasn't sure if an emigrant *left from* or an immigrant *came to*, and I wasn't sure which began with an *e* and which began with an *i*.

In other words, I had to know the difference between emigrating from the land of losers in order to immigrate into the winner's circle.

So I gambled.

Immigrant, I said, I-M-M-I-G-R-A-N-T. Immigrant.

When the news came over the intercom that I'd won the spelling bee and would go on to represent Whittle Springs Middle School at the district competition, I was rewarded with pats on the back and shoulder rubs. There were also catcalls against Section 8B, and I soon realized my peers in 8A had bested 8B by *proxy,* meaning: they didn't really care so much that I'd won but felt—especially the jocks—that my win was their victory too. I let them have it.

The district bee was held at the Alumni Memorial Building on the University of Tennessee campus. Mama, Granddaddy, Uncle Joe, and his wife, Dwen, came to cheer me on.

Inside the auditorium, the chairs were filled with dozens of my competitors. Granddaddy—Mama and Uncle Joe's father—sensing my nervousness, placed a hand on my shoulder to calm me.

My own daddy couldn't be there, and it was probably for the best. He was something of a *rogue,* a description of unknown origin, meaning: who knew what made him a rascal, a scoundrel? As in: if ever Daddy had exhibited *rogue* behavior, it would've been when he made knuckle prints in the cement wall of our apartment in Lonsdale and crushed his hand in the process. And it was seeing my mother's purple lip, a touch of pink where the underflesh bloomed through the bruise, that scared me, made me wonder how long the scars would last, if Mama would be able to continue her daily routine, saying nothing while she opened the mail, loaded the laundry, smoothed the wrinkles from my pants before she ironed them.

I wondered how my touch would feel to her after the bones of my daddy's hand had been seared into her face—if she would fear me too.

———

Predisposition. After the postclassical Latin *praedispositio,* meaning: a propensity in a person to respond or react in a certain way; a preexisting tendency to suffer from a disease or medical condition. As in: after my parent's divorce, my daddy became a man with a *predisposition* for walking in the rain without an umbrella from his new apartment in the projects to the liquor store a few blocks away, deeper in the projects, explaining that doing so was one of few ways he could get closer to God. Folks dismissed him and said he was faithful to the divine because he was so faithful to the liquor, which turned him into a man who often suffered seizures—*delirium tremens*—when he went too long without it and needed to borrow five dollars but would gladly accept a pocketful of change to help get himself a bottle.

The lights on the stage burned our faces as we waited our turns at the microphone. I'd made it three rounds and anticipated the fourth, searching the audience for my family in the dark. I'd expected Granddaddy to whistle between the space in his teeth after each successful round, but Mama probably warned him against it.

Unlike the spelling bees at Lonsdale Elementary and Whittle Springs Middle Schools, the district bee was set up professionally, a legitimate precursor to nationals: a table of judges, a pronouncer, a bell.

Your word is *parochial,* the pronouncer said.

As soon as I heard it, I was afraid this word would send me out; it would expose me as a fraud. And why would it not? A few weeks before, I had been invited, along with two other spellers, to appear on Channel Ten's *Live at Five.* The segment showcased us as "masterful spellers," but the first three words the host asked—*cuirassier, eudaemonic, terebinthinate*—stumped all of us. The fourth, *xenophobia,* I knew exactly how to spell. Just like it sounds, I thought. So I volunteered to spell it. I stared into the camera and said Z-E-N-O-P-H-O-B-I-A.

The host responded, Okay, so that was another tough one. And he decided there was no need to go on any further with the segment.

As I stood on stage contemplating how to spell *parochial*, I stalled for time, hoping for a gift, whatever that looked like, as I murmured the word, as if doing so was akin to an extended hand beseeching some small mercy, a simple act of grace to keep me from having to repeat those same syllables over and again, and there would soon arrive a respite in the form of a more accessible vocabulary, of words more suitable for the occasion, any one of them I could choose to substitute for *parochial*: *paralysis, procrastinate, predictable, Pinocchio*. Yes, these were the words that would prove I was a good speller, that I was worthy of standing before these strange figures shifting out there in the dark, and also the ones behind me who sat in their chairs lit up under the too-bright stage lighting, waiting to see just how far my aptitude would carry me. But why *parochial*? Where had that word even come from for me to know to commit it to memory? I was not one of those kids who *trained* for these events, who bypassed normal school activities to load up on etymologies or primary lexical units. Why should I need to know the origins of *parochial*? Or to know that a word that sounds like it begins with *z* actually begins with *x*?

Could you use *parochial* in a sentence? I asked.

I don't recall what sentence the pronouncer used, but he might as well have said: Though devoted to his *parochial* duties, he found time to begin his principal work, *The History of Greece*.

I had no idea what this word meant, much less how to spell it. Granddaddy, the king of Scrabble, knew. He'd prove it after the competition was over, as he'd proven his knowledge for so many other words, like *chivalric*, meaning: of or pertaining to *chivalry*. As in: Granddaddy sat, a beacon of *chivalric* grace, in a darkened theater ready to take my place if he would've been allowed to save his first-born grandson from sweating under the stage lights. Or, *telepathic*, meaning: he stared with great concentration, willing me to buck up, his competitive streak getting the better of him, and like the middle school jocks of Section 8A, he too would have taken a win, even by proxy.

Uncle Joe, Granddaddy's second-to-youngest child, was equally driven. He had graduated from Austin-East High School, which Mama had also attended, and which I would, too, in the fall as a freshman. Uncle Joe had been a popular scholar-athlete who helped lead his football team to a state championship when he was only a sophomore. His senior year, the entire student body voted him Mr. Austin-East. As I struggled with the word, I could almost hear his plaintive *dern*—he wasn't one to curse—knowing the inevitable loomed. Though, unlike Granddaddy, I couldn't imagine Uncle Joe wanting to save me from failure. His philosophy was live and learn, as in: At least now you know how to spell *parochial*, he'd later tell me.

Design. From the Middle French *desain, desaing, desseign,* meaning: fulfillment of a prearranged plan; an ultimate goal or purpose. As in: what were we supposed to learn in the course of this competition, the grand *design* that would alter our futures for the better if we could master the etymology and correct spellings of words? Were there life lessons in the vocabulary, in the individual letters that comprised the language we used to communicate so that we might understand something more about ourselves and the world we lived in by insisting on committing to memory words like *irrevocable,* which comes from the Latin *irrevocābilis,* meaning: cannot be revoked, repealed, annulled, or undone; that which is unalterable, irreversible? As in: one day, the news of Uncle Joe's cancer diagnosis would arrive, *irrevocable,* in Mama's face as she stood in the doorway to my bedroom, watching as I labored at the computer attempting to write a poem, a story, an essay, finding it difficult to process, when she said that her brother had cancer, meaning: her brother was dying.

Mama said *cancer,* and I thought the astrological sign.

Mama said *cancer,* and my mouth watered, thinking about a steamed feast of Alaskan king crab legs dipped in butter.

Mama said *cancer*, and my skin shuddered, imagining a disease you could catch by fucking without a condom.

Mama said *cancer*, and I knew we somehow needed to pretend that nothing had changed—dinner was still at eight, the grandchildren still needed their baths, and people we didn't even know were laughing together while dancing to their favorite songs alone at home in their living rooms.

And then there was Uncle Joe's wife, Dwen. When he died, we wondered how she was getting along without him. Was she hungry or thirsty for a glass of water, able to unwrap herself from her deceased husband's afghan to go into the kitchen to make a sandwich, leaning against the counter in the half-dark, nibbling deliberately like a small mouse, her ear cocked to every minor noise and echo as if she had only a slight chance of vanishing?

We worried she'd be overwhelmed with unannounced visitors—mostly family and friends dropping by after work with their small talk—wishing they would leave so she could pour herself a whiskey and sit in silence while the funeral flowers wilted, desperate for water.

———

I think I might have heard the bell ring, felt the tinny reverberations, even before I said, P-A-R-O-C-K-I-U-L, then turned away from the microphone, exiting the stage as I repeated once more, parockiul.

Mama, Granddaddy, Uncle Joe, and Dwen were already out of their seats, standing alongside the wall midway up the aisle, waiting for me.

P-A-R-O-C-H-I-A-L, Granddaddy said. Remember, *ch* can also make a hard *k* sound.

———

Vaticinate. From the Latin *vāticināt-*, meaning: to foretell, predict, prognosticate, or prophesy (a future event). As in: we walked out of the Alumni Memorial Building into a gray afternoon, which might've been a good omen, like rainy weather on one's wedding day, that would *vaticinate* how six years later, I'd be back in that building again when I transferred from Tennessee State University to the University of Tennessee to study creative writing because—as the blackboys on the playgrounds of my youth predicted—I was indeed a gay blackboy and therefore had no intention of sharing that experience in poems and short stories on an HBCU campus pulsing with black students whom I was so deathly afraid would reject me because of the content of those poems and short stories. So I escaped to the presumed safety of the liberal white creative writing classroom, where

I couldn't give a damn one way or another how or what the whiteboys and girls thought of my black gay ass, which is how I thrived—participating in a community that brought me back to that same auditorium stage to hear Gloria Steinem deliver a lecture, and afterward, stand in line at the microphone to ask her what she meant by the *melting pot*; and a few months later, Lucille Clifton would read her poetry as I clutched in a sweaty hand a copy of *Blessing the Boats* I waited for nearly an hour for her to sign.

On graduation day, Mama, Uncle Joe and Dwen, and other members from both sides of the family, gathered in Thompson-Boling Arena, texting to tell me where I could find them among all the other celebrants filling the arena with an overwhelming din of excitement.

Granddaddy wasn't there, but when I pursued an MFA at the University of Texas in Austin, I resurrected him in poems about how he sometimes sat leisurely in the early morning hours, eating a plate of peppered cucumbers and tomatoes glazed with oil and vinegar; how he told stories to his grandchildren about singing "The Lord's Prayer" on the radio and hitting a high C.

I wrote of his love for words, like *transfiguration*, meaning: an exalting, glorifying, or spiritual change. As in: after he died, my grief would not allow me to accept that Granddaddy's death was no sad occasion but a homegoing celebration, his earthly body in the throes of *transfiguration*, and so I crept through one of the windows in his house, crossed the floor's dusty seams like a seasoned robber, slipped in and out of the rooms until I found his blue robe strewn across the kitchen countertop as if he'd thrown it in haste, the last act before his death. I traced the outside stitching, felt the cold silk against my fingertips, entered through the sleeves, bearing the weight of the robe on my back, swallowed up in it until it became the very skin hanging from his bones.

Incidental Music

And sometimes when I'm bored or lonely or have a bug up my ass and don't want to do anything productive, I put on some music and think about the five years I lived with my mama after returning home from Austin, Texas, because I'd lost my job after making up a flimsy excuse for thinking I had the day off when I didn't have the day off and it was my third strike and that was that.

I think about those little girls who used to live across the street from us, all so close in age, and how they always arrived home from school at three o'clock sharp, off the bus in a bumbling mass, so wild-haired I'd want to take the straightening comb off the stove burner myself and rake it through their tender heads and let their straightened-out hair drape down the nape of their necks like freshly laundered sheets hung on the line to dry.

Those girls were darling, truly… they exalted life by simply running across the street as the bus pulled away, twirling up the sidewalk toward their house, their backpacks slung across their shoulders, jackets unzipped to the cold January air when it was winter, or even in the later months of autumn when it really got crisp. They didn't worry about illness . . . they were just little girls arriving home from school, from a teacher standing at a dry-erase board preaching fractions with markers that squeaked like rusty hinges, equations written in multicolors—red, blue, green—to show how 2 x 2 equals 4 but not 2 x 3.

I'd watch them as if I'd never been a child myself, as if, at twenty-eight years old, I'd forgotten having ever possessed such bristling love for being so singularly *young*. How they stumbled over one another into the house, targeting their mama, perhaps pleading for peanut butter and jelly sandwiches, and not one of them bemoaning how they'd missed her those long hours away at school. Not a hug around her waist or tug at her arm to bend her down for a kiss, but certainly, if they were raised anything like I was, they at least washed their hands, hung their packs on hooks in their bedrooms, and sat at the table quietly as they could—all things they were supposed to do—so their mama wouldn't threaten to whup their ass for being too boisterous, even when she understood their demands

for food were how children behaved after they'd been away
learning all day. And then they were off, never allowed enough
time to play until they were exhausted on jungle gyms, from
jumping rope, Hula-Hooping, or hopscotch—you name it,
they wanted it and more.

And then they'd be home again, craving a predinner snack,
for their mama to fix it fast because outdoors was calling, the last
few hours before dark sloughed off and it would be homework
time and bath time, then pajama time and bedtime.

They'd get up early the next morning, their mama having
to lug them out of their dreams since, perhaps, they were
trying to remember them as they were happening—at least
that's how it was when I was a boy—and having to be heaved
from bed as gravity settled, rendering their bodies limp with
the weight of sleep. It made them a ratty bunch who couldn't
bear the light when their mama wrenched their clenched eyes
open, stood them up straight, their snarls dropping to the
floor, so they were encouraged to wake up.

Did they understand how to be loved like this? This
generation of girls?

Would they remember? Keep memories like bins filled
with their favorite toys they knew where to find when the
mood struck?

I could go on contemplating their lives, what they'd
amount to once they left that house and bid farewell to the

front lawn littered with playthings and worn-out furniture, to the cat they'd adopted because they didn't know what else to do about its scratching at the door each morning.

I wonder if they'd wade into adulthood in the same manner they had shared secrets with friends while the teacher's back was turned, the kind only a child can elevate to cosmic importance, their desire for mystery residing in the shallow end of the pool where it's safe to venture in, where there's no thought of possible danger, just the innocuous fun available only in childhood.

Though what, as grown women, would they think of those childhoods? That they had been good? That they, as little girls, had been polite and respectful?

I'd say yes, remembering one day in particular, when the three of them wandered over to my yard after winter's first snows canceled the first few days of school and asked if I liked snow, a question so intriguing I didn't know how to answer it.

They pressed their bodies into a drift at the edge of the yard—perhaps too close to the road—as if to imprint a permanent mark onto the earth. It's possible this could rank among the highlights of their entire lives if ever it occurred to them to remember these days as I do: those wintry babies, darlings who didn't care that the shallow indentations they made in the snow would eventually disappear.

Miscreant Joy

was thirty-five when I felt enough time had passed for me to return to the scene of a crime, to the neighborhood corner store whose dumpster, with my friend Wesley, I helped set fire to in my youth. It had since been remodeled so that its facade was one of exposed brick, its windows shimmering panes of glass protected with wrought iron. Very chic.

I entered to find it almost as it was nearly two decades before: canned pears, stewed tomatoes, ziplocked bags of cheese in the coolers. Still the same, except less dust or expired sell-by dates, nor, I suspected, weevils in the cereal boxes. Just glint and evolution.

Inside, I didn't know what to do with my hands, so I clasped them above my head because, technically, I was against the law being there, walking the aisles.

The owner was still the same.

There was gum like the brand I stole as a kid in eighth grade at 6:00 a.m. when I should've been waiting for the school bus. I bet it was fresher, no stale Chiclets to bring on such terrible headaches like they used to do when I chewed it. The pain would put me to sleep by the time I got to class, and teachers would detain me after school for placing my head down on my desk, and so I'd miss the school bus and have to walk the long way home for chewing stolen, stale gum. I used to worry that arriving home from school so late would anger my daddy, but it never did, unlike Wesley's daddy who was so prone to anger and perhaps would've knuckle-gripped his son's face and blackened his eyes the way he did when Wesley started that fire; he knew no other use for his hands.

A beating like this wasn't a one and done deal. Perhaps that is why Wesley wanted to torch the dumpster in the first place, to be like his daddy, to use his hands to ignite the odor of sulfur, the trash crackling and sending up shit-smelling fumes, the dumpster's paint peeling from its sides like sunburned skin.

Perhaps Wesley never felt so in charge of his life as he did then, watching ash float like feathers into the sky above the alley. He seemed to feel so much joy that day with so much singeing around him. He'd done *this* and wanted to take it further: a match to the store's side paneling kissed with gasoline he'd pilfered from home, that he stored in a soda pop bottle in his back pocket.

And he would've, too, had I not walked away, had a police cruiser not come creeping down the alleyway.

And how he tore around the corner with the life draining from his face. I'd never seen a blackboy so pale.

He'd dared to procure for himself some semblance of joy that day. An early moon had risen over the oak trees, behind a sun vanishing from the horizon, yet it still glowed without being seen, a premonition Wesley wanted to match.

But that all changed when the siren and circling lights rounded the corner after him.

They eventually found their way to my house too. Wesley wouldn't go down for this alone. I may have walked away, but I had still been there to bask in the flames right alongside him. The difference is, at least then, I knew when to quit. But not Wesley.

When I left the store, I wondered if the owner remembered me: my head tilted back to whistle as my hands rummaged through empty pockets as they did the cardboard boxes of candies and gums all those years before. What if he did recall that boy, now a man, who'd come home for what, redemption?

Had he forgiven me?

Would this be the moment I'd turn to in the big book of my life when I needed, once more, a kind and subtle gesture to reassure me of the existence of absolution?

I wouldn't know entirely until I'd left the store, adjusting to the bright light reflecting off the windshields outside, when I could see that even the lampposts were newly polished. The neighborhood, now a palette of trees and greener grass and houses glamorized in their austere colors, was nothing like how I remembered it.

I hadn't noticed any of this when I first entered the store. Such is life, I suppose, that which in an instant changes from harsh to beautiful.

Part II

NOBODY HAS TO KNOW

Mother, do you know
I roam alone at night?
I wear colognes,
tight pants, and
chains of gold,
as I search
for men willing
to come back
to candlelight.

—Essex Hemphill
"In the Life"

Say Uncle

'd been browsing the hook-up site Adam4Adam on my laptop when my niece came up suddenly behind me, exclaiming, Uncle!

I snapped the screen down and looked over my shoulder, searching her face, determining how to respond to her set jaw and wide eyes. Not even a simple *What?* seemed sufficient. So I said nothing. She walked around to face me, then to the door, where, outside, the sound of the ice cream truck inching down the street made its way to our house, its jingle faint and incomprehensible. My niece stared back at me and again said, Uncle! with such excitement I clutched the laptop and clenched my teeth inside my closed mouth. And because I was a rational person with a graduate degree, I didn't think to ask, What did you see? but instead assumed that she wanted to know why I was childless, why I'd provided no cousins for her or her sisters, no nieces or nephews for my own siblings, no grandchildren for my mama and daddy.

Uncle, she said again.

Would you like to help load the dishwasher? I asked, but she clearly wasn't satisfied.

Uncle, she said as if to ask a question, insisting. She tapped a bony finger against her lip as if she knew a secret.

She said, Uncle, as though it were my preternatural station in life, the way a bridesmaid was always a bride's maid, or the way single men with male companions were both called "Uncle" when their families gathered for Sunday dinners, barbecues, or reunions. She looked at me with Dora the Explorer eyes. Uncle, she said, her voice scaling toward the upper register of the staff, this time intoning an apparent question she seemed already to know the answer to.

Never end sentences in prepositions . . . or is it *with* prepositions? I told her, and she studied me as if she were an Encyclopedia Brown for the Justin Bieber generation because I was speaking in non sequiturs.

Uncle, she said, without ever following through with a predicate, suggesting I knew where this was going, an accusation dividing syllables into equal parts, *Un-cle*.

I thought back to when she was an infant, of holding her tiny body flush against my chest just moments after she was born. Then, she startled so suddenly in my arms; my grip having loosened, she must have felt certain of slipping to the floor and so she jerked.

Every mother present in that room reached as one, demanded that I hand the child over. Even then she incited fear in me. And now, Uncle was all she'd say. And what else could I do except cup her chin in my palm and draw her gaze away?

I wasn't married, no girlfriend.

Uncle, she said, until the living room we were in became a gallery of journalists and paparazzi, a judge poised to swing the gavel, and a jury skeptical of my every movement.

What were my hands doing? Had my eyebrows lifted too far, become too arched?

Uncle, she repeated.

Mt. Vesuvius in a sundress destroying Pompeii.

Uncle, she said, tempting me to pour a shot of rum from the bottle beneath the kitchen sink.

Uncle. Chase it with beer.

Uncle. Bring on inebriation as if my head were filled with cumuli, a soft rain falling like spring water over stones, soothing.

Uncle. I just might risk drunkenness for the chance it would silence her tongue.

Uncle, she said, as when she wanted a jelly sandwich or a grilled cheese or a bounce on the trampoline in the neighbor's backyard.

Uncle, she said, nodding her head to the sound of "Row, Row, Row Your Boat" that had been blaring from the ice cream truck's bullhorn for all those many Uncles.

Of course!

I pulled a five-dollar bill from my pocket, and she took it swiftly out the door.

I wouldn't see her again until evening, when I called her in, when she stood half-inside the house, pleading Uncle to stay outdoors since there was still a sliver of daylight left.

Nobody Has to Know

I couldn't get enough of straight men, and so, for a while, I pursued only them. And to be clear, I don't mean straight-*acting*, since too often those types failed to keep up appearances. But I wanted *him*, the one who felt he had everything to lose if gossip got back to his wife or girlfriend that something was amiss with her man; yes, he had to have long-term female companionship and children, of course. Being a daddy was a must. I wanted him in church on Sunday mornings, fearing what the congregation might say about his betrayal of what had been written down in the Word if it were ever discovered that he—*Yes, can you believe it? The shame of it all!*—had those *unseemly urges*. I wanted him absolutely apoplectic at the mere thought of signaling to another man in public that he was interested—even if deftly sly—and proving it with a knowing glance, a suggestive nod, or a hand gesture, the usual rubbing of the palms together with an attendant grin, a stroke of a clean-shaven chin with long fingers or a scratching at his beard or whiskers, all the varieties of manual signposting that foretold *yes, you there* . . . he should instead save his attentions for the privacy of untraceable meeting places, where it was safest and he needn't worry about the loathsome sleuthing of so many nosy minds insisting on knowing the missing part of his story, those eager to become privy to what lurked there locked behind his eyes, cowering— an unsolvable riddle—where something grave peered back at them, blank like slate or tombstone chipping away.

And why was it always into the eyes that we cast down our buckets to draw information about whether someone *is* or *isn't?* Why not search the hands, which may bear the markings of minimal labor, as if simply from a responsibility to rise from bed each morning? Judge from that if one must.

Should a man indeed be gay, or if he be a straight man who enjoys fucking or being fucked by another man, then let him relinquish his head, the kink of dense, coarse hair in which fingers may tread down to the scalp to get to the crown at the center. Remove the crown, and the same-sex loving self will fall from his skin, roll in dirt, dip in water—a new casing entombed, embalmed with new life.

And with this new life, allow him mystery without acknowledging the ghostlier self. Let him appear to the world as if from a window, waiting for a time when and for whom he will open a door, cross a threshold, or remain locked inside, indefinitely, for the sake of himself.

I remember it well, that moment of clarity when I felt my life was better served in the closet, a form of self-preservation that needn't undermine my self-esteem. It was all a matter of the cost benefit analysis: the struggle to either reconcile my same-sex attraction in public or face rebuke that could certainly take an emotional, psychological toll but also a physical one.

I thought of Aaron Price, the Morehouse student who, on November 3, 2002, used a bat to fracture the skull of Gregory Love, a fellow student, music major, and member of the glee club, for allegedly looking at him in the shower. Love claimed he thought he'd seen his roommate—he wasn't wearing his glasses—so the incident became one of mistaken identity but also of gay panic.

A lot of people believe that Love deserved to get beaten up if he was looking in the shower stall, said one Morehouse student to the *Atlanta Journal-Constitution*.

And so, if the attack was indeed justified by the victim's perceived sexual advance, was it like sex, then, the way the bat caused Gregory Love to bend and writhe beneath water pouring from a shower head, rivulets of his blood flowing between the cracks of the tile?

Or was it like music?

I could only imagine him in the stall, tingling to the very edges of his skin. Symphony of dissonant violins in his ear and every syncopated beat was conducted by hands wielding a bat. Gregory's arms and legs twitching like eighth notes, his heart beating in his chest like thirty-seconds, his mouth whimpering grace notes.

When it ended, was there afterglow, a cadence to this opus?

What happened to the music? Where did it go when the player and his instrument evaporated into steam and haze?

And what warranted the murder of Gwen Amber Rose Araujo, a Latina teen beaten and strangled to death on October 4, 2002, when her murderers—Jason Cazares, Michael Magidson, José Merél, and Jaron Nabors, with at least two of whom she had sexual encounters—discovered she was transgender? Was it trans panic they experienced, or did they believe that she had raped them, forced them into homosexual acts unwittingly, through deception, which then justified their decision that she had to die, to be placed in a pickup truck and driven four hours away to be buried near the Sierra Nevada mountains in a shallow grave in the El Dorado National Forest?

And in their four-hour drive back home, or perhaps while bonding over a McDonald's breakfast to satiate another hunger—or it may have been in the details of their blood pact, or quite possibly even as any of them slipped into bed—did a single one of them save in their memories the wet dark boughs' skeletal looming against the gemstone sky?

Did they recall whether there were birds perched on leafless branches, singing a weeping chorus?

Did anyone notice if forest creatures gathered in a moonlight procession behind Gwen's body as it was dragged across the wooded floor, a halo of leaves and needles collecting around her head?

Were they content she never felt the slick black grass against her cheeks?

Did they wonder—even in death—if her eyes saw past shadows, beyond whirling fists and shovels, into the evil of men?

When her bulk shuddered the grave they dropped her in, did they inherit the fear she would no longer feel yet keeps coming and coming and coming?

———

And so by the time I was nineteen, I was desperate to become a black gay man who could not only pass for straight but also one whom it would never occur to anyone that I wasn't. But this mission was doomed to failure. For example, no straight man on the down low would risk being caught in a discreet corner of a bookstore, skimming through *Ceremonies* by Essex Hemphill, a black gay poet. But there I was, in one such corner, reading one of his poems, "American Hero," and getting aroused by images of a man shooting a basketball, who insists on aiming at the hole to let the tension go.

I was enthralled by his words, which suggested that I aspired to get ass, that we all should, and that we should whistle for it, applaud it, and shout vulgarities as we were getting it. "This," Hemphill wrote, "is how you hook the boy who makes slaves out of men."

But what did I know about actual—not pillow-talk-pretend—sex with men, of loving them?

I was so green, I was an endless field of grass, a forest of evergreens. Green at the gills, which meant, yes, I was sometimes prone to panic and became nauseated from the uncertainty of a man's response to my advancements.

"I go to the place where danger awaits me." Hemphill was prone to the strange boy he passed on street corners, lingering to glimpse a face shrouded too deeply in shadow, hoping to persuade him to better light before either of them thought it was best to give up and go on his way.

"I go to the place where the good feelin' awaits me, self-destruction in my hand." Both Hemphill and the strange boy would give a double take before they both doubled back.

Overwhelmed by curiosity, wanting that closer look, they slowed their pace until the gap between them shrank to mere inches.

But if they met each other in the place where self-destruction resides, would romance even be possible? What was happening in their faces, in what that dim flickering in their eyes foretold, where there once used to be a bright shine, a milky white that enriched the color of their irises, and at the center was a marble of an impeccable hue?

That brilliance had diminished, leaving only what lust had tarnished when the two of them fucked but never made love.

They may have kissed, but they never brushed the back of a hand across the other's cheek.

They may have dared to hold hands, but they were more content to be two warm bodies, silent in a bed.

What did this mean for me? Was it sex or romance? I was nineteen years old, cowering in the corner of a bookstore in downtown Nashville, careful of curious minds who might somehow learn this thing about me because of this book I held at my fingertips.

If someone were to ask, *What are you reading?* I'd have to slip quickly through the slender aisles like a man who'd lost his mind, holding *Ceremonies* loosely at arm's length, as if at any moment, I'd let it fall to the ground so I could get the hell out of there.

But I wanted the book. I only needed to pay. And go.

I approached the counter, my eyes averted, and pushed the book forward with the barcode facing up, so the gay associate behind the register inside the gay bookstore in the gay district of downtown Nashville wouldn't think for a moment that I too might be gay, because he'd be minding his own business. He'd think I was extremely conscientious to have the barcode ready to scan, and I'd pay, and he'd package my purchase, though not in one of those thin, tan bags meant for magazines that end up hidden beneath mattresses or behind chests of drawers but a grocery bag with handles I could use at the nearby farmers market to hold apples and bananas, grapes or oranges or peaches, so no one would ever think that inside the bag, among the fruit, was a book whose cover had a photo of a half-naked black man exposed to his midriff, all abdomen, pectorals, and biceps fleshed into a statuesque pose, his right arm raised perpendicular to his body, his palm turned toward the sky, his head tilted back with dreadlocks flung wildly into the air as if he'd just given them a vigorous shake and was now frozen in time.

I had to conceal my attraction to this man's body, not only from the clerk to whom I presented the barcode—who placed it inside a black plastic bag, who smiled and told me to come back so he might suggest other titles of interest to me—but also from everyone else, which meant I would read the clerk's recommendations on guard and always with my back against a wall.

Omar

He was nineteen, like me. A sophomore at Tennessee State University with the smoothest brown skin, a shaved head, and pretty pink lips he liked to lick wet. I wanted so badly to fuck him.

I wasn't brave enough, though, to walk through the Jack and Jill bathroom that joined our two rooms and knock on his door just to say hello or to contrive an excuse, to tell him I'd heard he was interested in joining my fraternity or to ask him if he had an extra pair of batteries to replace the dead ones in my remote control.

I wouldn't tell him how he kept me tangled nights on end, restless in the sheets, my hands shoved inside my underwear, wondering if he might be doing the same, thinking of me as I did of him.

I was tempted to approach him one day when I went to use the bathroom and noticed the tile floor glowing from light that must have been coming from his open door, which normally he kept shut.

Was this a sign?

Since I needed to use the bathroom, I'd have to close his door, which might initiate a conversation.

I could apologize for disturbing him.

He might apologize for leaving the door open, and I'd tell him it was no problem.

He'd complain that it'd gotten so damn hot and he'd only wanted to circulate the breeze coming in through the open window.

I'd want to ask him what he enjoyed getting into when it got as hot as this, but I'd likely be too embarrassed to say such a thing and tell him instead that the breeze did feel good and leave it at that.

I also could have said nothing and simply watched him sit at a desk with an open book, wearing sweatpants and no shirt, his elbow propped so his head rested in the palm of his hand as he read. Everything in the room would be neat. He would make a note in the book, and I would notice, like me, he was left-handed.

If I were to have knocked on the door to tell him I needed to shut it to use the bathroom, then promised to crack it back open when I was finished, I'm sure I would have ruined nothing.

He might have shut the book, turned to face me, and offered to close the door himself just to be closer to me. I wouldn't avert my eyes, and neither would he.

But this would not be how it happened.

I just stood there, contemplating the open door.

This was as far as I would go.

I wouldn't be touched by him that night.

I wasn't even sure if Omar was his name.

———

Instead of getting to know him, I romanticized him to my best friends, Jerome and Marshall, suggesting there might be a mutual attraction when I told them how I left Hale Hall, our dorm, for class one day and saw Omar pimpin' toward me with his backpack slung over a shoulder, a hand tucked in the top of his jean pocket, looking very collegiate with his spectacles on.

I told them how I waited in the courtyard outside the dorm entrance because I couldn't leave just yet. Not until he was closer, until he passed by, and briefly, I was shoulder to shoulder with him and smelled the scent of Irish Spring.

I told them how I could only nod in response when he said 'Sup and slowed his pace.

I told them how I followed his eyes as they moved from top to bottom and then up again, as if he were taking stock of me.

That's trade right there, baby, Jerome said. I would eat those cakes forthwith.

Yes, honey, quite! Boy gets dowwwwn, Marshall said.

I didn't know much about what *trade* was, but I knew that *gets down* meant *secrets.*

Marshall and Jerome told me to beware those secrets. Told me to be suspicious of any blackboy, especially trade or *straight* boys who were too slim in build or who coughed without end or revealed track marks along their arm or had sores in their mouth.

If he was a top, I had less to worry about since the chances of him carrying HIV (or what we called the *ick*) were minimal, especially if he wasn't too keen on giving oral.

How would he catch it, through the urethra? Jerome joked.

If he were a bottom, I should examine his sphincter to ensure it was tight as a balloon knot; otherwise, if it yielded too easily to probing—an insertion of one or two fingers— then he was *hot*, a distinction that didn't mean extremely beautiful but dangerously promiscuous.

But if all checked out, I could take a blackboy to bed without any further questions.

But nothing would ever materialize between Omar and me. We'd go that entire year, barely whispering a word to one another. If anything, we gave him short shrift, made him a cautionary tale without any evidence he was someone to worry over. Nevertheless, Jerome issued one final warning about trade: Never let him cum inside you.

Love, Like in the Movies

'be been thinking about my first adolescent crush, who
he might've been among the roughneck, drug-dealing
fuckboys who posted on street corners like traffic signs in
the Lonsdale projects. He was an older blackboy, dropped
out of high school, who kept a low profile with his crew in
the alley across from Sam E. Hill Primary, and he sat on the
hood of a broken-down car in a wifebeater and low-hanging
jeans, boxers bunched around his waist, passing around joints
and forties of malt liquor, getting his jollies by bragging to his
homeboys about all the women he'd fucked or the niggas he'd
shot, before they all migrated to Pascal Drive to circumvent,
if not outright test, the community's moral convictions by
selling dope too close to First Calvary Baptist Church like
a pack of sacrileges. I fail to conjure a name, a face; he's just
a composite figure of the many blackboys who once entered
into my waking and dreaming consciousness like relics of a

bygone past that even then they were already becoming. I'm curious to know who he is because I want to recreate some romantic notion of what might've taken place between two blackboys dramatically different in age and experience after having watched Luca Guadagnino's *Call Me by Your Name* for what has to be the seventy-fifth time, replaying the scene when Oliver says to Elio, Call me by your name, and I'll call you by mine, the two of them lying together in bed, their skin pale in the powdery light of a bright moon so that it appears to be the blue hour before dawn yet it is still night. They face one another nose to nose. Oliver whispers his instructions. Elio at first looks taken aback, but he capitulates and says his name—Elio—and points to Oliver as if to say, *like this?* Oliver reciprocates, O-li-ver, heavy with the breath that speaks it. They say their names again; Elio grabs Oliver by the chin to kiss his lips; they roll away together out of frame before the scene dissolves.

————

You'd think this is my favorite scene in the film, but it isn't. My favorite is actually the sequence that begins with a series of crosscuts that show Oliver and Elio performing separate actions that are happening simultaneously. The crosscutting creates tension that is at once suspenseful, intimate, and awkward. We first see Oliver arriving to Elio's family's villa

after a bicycle ride. It is late morning or early afternoon—
the sunshine is so bright, who can really tell what time of
day it is? Oliver dismounts, jumping backward off the bike
as it continues traveling forward, but he quickly grabs the
seat to stop it. (It's an extremely skillful move.) He wears an
unbuttoned, blue oxford shirt, which bares his hairy chest
and billows with each stride he makes toward the house. Then
the film cuts to Elio alone, lying in bed. He checks his watch;
a book is discarded beside him as if out of boredom. He places
a hand behind his head, and the other slides inside his boxer
shorts. Cut back to Oliver, who is now using the shirt to swab
the sweat from his body as he approaches—even closer—the
villa's entrance. He is almost out of frame when we cut to Elio
again. In three separate shots (from three different angles)
we see him slide his hand in and out of his boxers, staring
into space as if conjuring an image. The camera lingers on
the third shot, a closer view of him with his hand inside his
underwear, massaging. . . . Suddenly, there's a knock at his
door, and Oliver barges into the room, perhaps in time to see
Elio yank his hand from his boxers and struggle to pick up
the book and open it. Elio braces himself on an elbow, props
up a leg to hide his crotch.

Elio, what are you doing? Oliver says.

Reading.

How come you're not with everyone else down by the river?

I have an allergy, Elio says, gesturing around his mouth and nose to indicate he has an allergy.

Oliver looks intently at Elio.

Yeah, me too, he says. Maybe we have the same one.

Here, Oliver is either (1) telling the truth, (2) indulging Elio so as not to humiliate him, or (3) using very subdued sarcasm to imply that yes, he has the same allergy as Elio if it's true that Elio was indeed reading a book when he entered the room. Whatever his intentions, Oliver says, Why don't you and I go swimming? *(But what about your allergy?)* Elio says, Right now? because right now he has an erection. Oliver clasps Elio's forearm. Yes, right now, he says and tries to pull him out of bed. Come on, Oliver insists, let's go. Elio relents and waits for Oliver to take two steps through the Jack and Jill bathroom that joins their rooms before he looks down, dismayed at his crotch, and slams his body repeatedly against the mattress as if Oliver couldn't possibly hear the ruckus of squeaky coil springs and what it might imply. Elio undresses and shows off his I-definitely-have-a-seventeen-year-old-whiteboy booty, then peeks into Oliver's room, nearly gagging—as if he's never seen such things—when Oliver pulls a pair of red trunks over the curve of his firm white ass.

See you downstairs, Oliver says, leaving Elio to stare at his own reflection in the bathroom mirror.

In *Call Me by Your Name*, revelations take the form of innuendo that must often be read between the lines. A simple question asked at the top of the scene (Elio, what are you doing?) isn't an instance of small talk but rather a point of tension, a turn in the plot that baits us as we anticipate what comes next, maneuvering us through the crafty flirtations and shifting power dynamics until we are brought ultimately to the end of the scene, where Elio and Oliver are picking apricots. With all the space in the world to select from an abundance of fruit, Elio decides to home in on the lower-hanging apricots. He uses his forearm to ease (or tease) Oliver out of his way to reach them, slowly pushing him the maximum distance away while still allowing his touch to linger on Oliver's body. But this is no rebuff. Elio wants to regain the control he once had. Or perhaps he has decided to answer Oliver's question—*What are you doing?*—in a more tangible way by finding communion with his body, by saying to Oliver, in effect, *I'm letting you know.*

———

In the novel on which the film is based, Elio compares, at some length, Oliver's ass to a peach. I was no different in the admiration I had for those older blackboys in sagging jeans, basketball shorts, or sweatpants exposing asses that sat high on their thighs, not like pieces of fruit but like a pair of globes stretching the fabric of boxers or tighty-whities.

But what adolescent blackboy growing up in the projects of Knoxville has the audacity of an Elio to openly marvel at another blackboy's physical attributes, much less to know what to do with them?

If an adolescent blackboy in the projects recognized this attraction, it became essential he learned to tend to his blooming carnality carefully.

Except the older blackboys probably never noticed they'd become the object of a young blackboy's fantasies. So they paid him no mind. And soon enough, the young blackboy would realize this as well. Transference would become his enemy as, naturally, he would start to harbor feelings for blackboys his own age. And being in such proximity, it became difficult to hide those feelings from them.

And what happened if the other blackboys were to find out? Then the adolescent blackboy from the projects might become a victim of the cruelest majority: bullied by his own peers. And what exactly might he do to draw their wrath? It might have nothing to do with whether he was crushing on one of them or not.

Perhaps he was overly fond of singing.

Perhaps he had a little twist in his step.

A lisp in his talk.

Perhaps the hallways would become crowded with sneers and jeers, someone tripping him every chance they had, flicking narrow fingers against his skull, nicking his head with clippers they'd brought in from home, intending for him to resemble a mangy dog.

Perhaps they'd call him *mangy dog* among other names: *bitch, faggot, dicklicker.*

Perhaps it'd be stenciled on his locker as if it were protest graffiti, bringing him to his knees, elbow deep in suds, scrubbing off the words, filtering all his *whys* and *what-did-I-dos* through wrung-out rags and sponges.

Perhaps he'd avoid them by walking home after school each day instead of riding the bus, even in the cold months, bunched up in his winter coat, shivering for miles with his head bent to the wind, cinching his coat tighter, adjusting the soreness from his shoulders each time he switched his book bag from one side to the other, struggling to make it home—because all he wanted was to make it home—and meanwhile, those boys would pass by him, hanging out the bus windows, screaming, Shake the gay away! so uncontrollably content in their miscreant joy they might not ever recover from it.

And then what?

Perhaps he grew up and went away to college, where he thought it might be safe (or at least safer) to allow his adolescent attractions to mature until he eventually let another blackboy into his bed. And after some time, they began to feel something like love for one another, a new sensation neither could quite explain, though each of them understood it must be experienced in secret.

Perhaps the bullying followed him there, to college, and his not-yet-understood emotion was discovered and shared across campus, which shamed him back into those middle school hallways, back onto the long road he walked home alone, back to where he felt there was nothing he could do to keep out the cold.

And what if this became too much and he disappeared himself miles away from anyone who knew him, found himself on a bridge on a day when the sky turns mauve at dusk, the way it sometimes does when fall approaches, when the wind is a trifle breezier, when clouds stretch into one long brow along the horizon?

What if he placed one hand over the other to balance his knees on the rails but struggled with his footing because he couldn't see, because he was crying so hard?

What if he rested a hand at the nape of his neck, felt in his palm a greasy veneer of sweat, an oil slick of fear and ambition sliding down his back?

What if he breathed with the insistence of a gymnast about to take on the pommel horse, which was how he might've composed himself before lifting one leg, then the other, over the rail to ease his heels onto the margin, his toes pointed perpendicular to the water below?

What if there was only enough room to wipe his face without falling, just yet, so that he might gather his wits to do this with dignity?

What if, when he was nearly ready, he cloistered in a nook he'd sidestepped several paces to find?

What if he thought of his mother sweeping the floors of the house as she did every day at that time, of how he'd wanted so much to make her proud?

What if, more than anything, he wanted to do this better than all those who'd failed before him?

What if he considered how the wind might gather inside his shirt, make him aerodynamic when he didn't want to fly, and so removed it?

What if he was deliberate even through the tears in his eyes, figuring how to wrap his body around a pole that plunged to the bottom of the river, inching his way methodically to the top as if he understood the minute particulars of geometry, physics, and calculus, climbing and climbing until his way up equated with how he would end up below?

What if he wondered if the river would shatter when he broke the surface, if he'd crumble like an ancient cathedral or sink in slow motion while fish circled him like a maypole?

What if, before he leaped, he assured himself the world would be just fine without him, and he without it, and that things would get back to their normal course in due time, the way, once he crashed through the water, the surface of the river would appear as if it had never been anything but this peaceful wrinkling?

————

Perhaps the reason I can't recall my first adolescent crush is because he didn't exist in the same way that we witness Elio and Oliver crushing on, then falling in love with, one another. Even when I longed for it. For a blackboy growing up in the projects like me, perhaps the stakes were too high for it to be possible. Not so in *Call Me by Your Name*. No one is threatened or bullied. The only nemesis is time. We are meant to thirst over Timothée Chalamet and Armie Hammer—that is, Elio and Oliver—performing their slow-burning love affair over the course of six weeks in the summer of 1983 somewhere in the bucolic countryside of northern Italy. For two hours and twelve minutes, beginning with the opening credit sequence set to John Adams's dueling pianos ("Hallelujah Junction") and Elio's waggish remark (*L'usurpateur!*) upon Oliver's arrival to the Perlman family's Italian villa in the film's first scene, we sit enthralled until the very last frame, when we are overcome with solemnity, watching flickers of a crackling fire flash across Elio's face as he crouches before the flames, quietly fighting back the tears that will eventually fall, thinking of Oliver who is an ocean away, and, we are to presume, thinking of a love that is equally as deep if not tragically possible but once in a lifetime, or in an ephemeral summer. And even the film's final music—Sufjan Stevens's "Visions of Gideon"—doesn't forewarn us that their (our) story is over until the title displays and the credits begin to roll—yellow letters against the close-up of Elio's face—and we are gutted, yearning for love and to be loved, like in the movies.

No Strings Attached

LeShaun was a light-skinned (or redbone/high yellow) black man I met in an internet chatroom during my junior year in college. He was ten years my senior, thirty-one, with hooded eyes that made me swoon but never betrayed that he was also a married man on the down low.

His voice was soft but not effeminate, like a man who spoke normally with a deep, rich tone. But when vulnerable, his voice lightened, took on a subtle husky timbre that imbued him with a sensitivity that endeared me to him, and I found myself often smiling until my face hurt.

I loved to hear him talk. To watch his lips come together and part deliberately while enunciating his words, the way a man does when he knows the allure of his best features.

He had the smallest ears I'd ever seen on a man.

LeShaun wasn't exactly what I'd call trade, but he carried the same mystery as someone who was. Otherwise, he was a man very svelte and debonair in simple dark slacks and a shirt open at the collar, who wore designer cologne that tinged the air with a sweet scent that lingered long after he'd left.

He kept all the trappings of his success, his efficiency at maintaining secrecy in his life, hidden beneath the hood of his eyes.

He flew into Knoxville from some Midwest city I believed was probably Chicago or Detroit, but he would never tell me because he wanted to keep things simple. No complications, no need to stress when he promised to call me up when he was in town for business every other weekend, to let me know in person how much he missed the way I tasted.

He meant the way his breath issued warm against my neck, when he yearned to *rock the boat*, he'd say, because he was an old soul with a love for a little old-school rhythm and blues.

When I think of him now, I always remember our first in-person meeting, in my apartment. I invited him in, and he surveyed the living room, then asked me where the bedroom was. I pointed the way, and he led me down the hall.

I understood how he wanted things to go.

He stepped out of his shoes and socks, pulled down his pants and his underwear, tossing aside each article rather lazily. We both kept on our shirts, facing each other, then he moved away quickly toward my bedroom window to close the blinds, which probably should've happened before we

removed our clothes, but when he turned away from me, I
was glad the blinds were open. I took pleasure admiring his
lips, as I did his ass, the way his shirt—had he a flatter ass—
would've fallen unremarkably straight down his backside
but instead rested right there at the top of the curve, which
brought my eyes to his thick thighs, the tiniest hairs—almost
like a layer of dust—covering his taut skin.

We were both erect, and we gradually walked closer to
one another, his arm reaching out until his fingertips touched
my waist and crawled to my hipbone, urging me forward
until his hand curved around and rested at the small of my
back, a one-armed embrace that made him suck air through
his teeth when our bodies made contact.

He pushed me from behind, his head in the small of my
back, toward the bed, not letting go of my hips. I climbed on
the bed and slid backward until I rested against the wall, and he
crawled after me until he sat beside me, shoulder to shoulder. No
one spoke, especially me, for whom all of this was surreal, like a
page from an internet sex story I'd been reading occasionally, a
story that had become this script I was now enacting.

I reached over to the side table and handed him a bottle
of lotion. He squirted some in his hand and then in mine.
He crossed one leg over mine so that his thigh sat atop my
thigh, which brought him even closer, and we each took one
another's hard flesh in our hands.

He moaned *fuck*, over and over, drawing it out, *fuuuck*, teaching me how to pleasure him. Then his lips pressed against my lips, his tongue forceful and gentle at once.

I bit into his shoulder, his triceps, grazed his earlobe with my teeth, licked along the length of his neck while he worked to bring me to climax.

And I did. And then so did he.

Our breaths were heavy as we leaned back against the wall.

I took this moment to remember that he was married, that the entire time he was with me, he had a wife at home who was possibly standing at a sink, piling dirty dishes full to the rim after having spent a day cooking a recipe she'd found on the internet.

He was with me while she was planning to surprise this man, her husband, by recapturing with a simple dish how they had once dined *alfresco* in some city in Italy some years ago, perhaps on an anniversary; she wanted to remember which dishes he liked to have prepared *alla parmigiana*—eggplant, veal, or chicken?

And yet, I imagined myself playing house with him one day, encouraged by the things I knew his wife would let him do.

I hadn't yet let him penetrate me because deep down, I knew I shouldn't, that this might be taking things too far, that there was something wrong about all of this, that this would be a form of consummation that should be reserved only for her, for making babies.

But then I began to reconsider. He wanted me to be his something forbidden, his once-in-a-while satiation of his appetite. How could I possibly resist?

He had his urges, and I was down for the temptation, that flick of his tongue, that whispered, *How do you want it?* as he urged me to respond to that feeling inside my chest, of my heart sinking to my toes.

Except when he tried to penetrate me, I became overwhelmed by the pain and told him, Oh, no, not today.

He nudged my shoulder with his nose, spoke with his mouth pressed to my skin.

You can't give up on me now, he said.

I feared that if I didn't allow him soon, he might desert me, so I said I wanted to try it lying on my stomach (with his stomach and chest on my back so I could feel his heart beating almost in rhythm with his hips). This way I learned to relax, to coax him in slowly, tapping his thigh to signal when to stop, when to push on. Start, stop, until I no longer felt as if I were being pried apart but comforted by the gentle pressure, and then the mounting aggression when he sensed my body accepting more of him, until he was full on fucking me, even though if anyone were to ask, I'd say this was the day we made love for the first time.

As he continued to thrust inside me, I imagined the two of us taking a warm shower together afterward or snuggling in bed, feeding each other tater tots from Sonic—it had become our favorite spot—and trying not to drip ketchup on the sheets. Or we could go for something sweet, licking cake batter off each other's fingers. Yes, we could do any of those things, and I would be satisfied. I could have fantasies of the afterglow, and he could continue to thrust inside me and thrust inside me and thrust inside me.

When we were done, he wiped himself off with a towel, and I stared at him intently because it dawned on me, with a bit of humor, that he might be the lover-boy pillow of my childhood.

I experienced, too, apprehension that I might seem to him less a man—a faggot—by having been fucked by him, and though it was a weird occasion to bring this up, I sat on the bed in front of him as he relaxed, half-dozing with his head against the wall, and tried to explain this to him, saying that all my life, I'd sensed that folks had been trying to suss me out. He asked me what I meant, and because I couldn't say it plainly, I told him about how the schoolyard blackboys of my childhood used urban legends to trick me into believing my sexuality could be discovered on a playground by the way I reacted to their taunts.

I spoke to him of fluffy pink slippers and of my best friend, Maurice, shaming me with stories of his sexual conquests when he was a mere preteen.

LeShaun took my hand, his head tilted back, eyes still closed, and told me that I wasn't a faggot.

I know, he said, because I don't get down with faggots.

And then he was ready to fuck me again, and I suggested he use a condom this time. He turned me on my stomach and spread his body across the length of mine, nuzzled deep in the back of my neck, his voice muffled when he replied, You'll be aight. I'm clean. Only faggots need to use condoms, right?

He rolled off me when he finished. But unlike before, I felt the urge to use the toilet.

I sat straining, but nothing solid seemed to be passing, yet I definitely felt *something*. It was slippery, not exactly watery. Perhaps excess lubricant, I thought, emptying from my body?

I wiped myself; the toilet paper was damp but still white. And before I tossed the tissue, I looked inside the bowl and didn't understand what I saw there floating so strangely luminous and waxy, almost as if a lit candle had been dripping into the water.

I didn't know why exactly, at least initially, but a part of me wanted to return to him in bed to ask, only as a joke, Where did your cum go?

I didn't flush the toilet, though, until I could rid myself of the strange feeling in my gut.

I sensed that I was glimpsing a future that was taking shape right there before me, one that was evidence of what resulted when one's body with another's body gives and receives so much pleasure.

I wanted to believe that inside the toilet bowl was the sign of LeShaun's love, that it had burst through him and into me, and here it was, appearing like small, milky white opals clinging to the surface of the water.

When I returned to bed, I expected to find LeShaun asleep. He wasn't. He'd been waiting to pull me into bed. He had to leave early in the morning and slept more easily when he had me to hold in his arms.

Before I fell asleep, I promised to cook him a dinner that would rival the Italian cuisines he said his wife was so famous for.

He asked me never to talk about his wife and relaxed his hold around my body until I felt nothing except his warm breath against my back as we drifted off to sleep.

———

As promised, for his next visit, I prepared a meal of sautéed portobello mushrooms, scallions, garlic. Baked halibut, and shrimp tossed in brown butter.

I set the table with candles, a new set of dinner plates I bought on sale from Walmart.

I filled a Dutch oven with ice to chill my favorite sauvignon blanc, which I hoped he'd enjoy too.

I polished the wine glasses and the glasses for water.

I dimmed the lights and placed a few Anita Baker CDs in the carousel of my stereo and pressed Play.

I left the door slightly ajar so he'd smell the aromas immediately when he walked in.

I went outside after a while to wait for his car, mistaking each one that passed by for his.

I was confident it would only be a matter of time before LeShaun shifted his allegiance from his wife to me. I needed only to be patient, content with the current situation.

Except I had no reason in the world to put any faith in the idea.

I had figured out the rationalization, that surely he wouldn't remain trapped in his marriage. He'd have his children, one after another. And his life would move forward.

Eventually he would have raised them, and this would be the turn of the tide.

There would be the quiet house, he and his wife begrudging one another with casual touches, kisses against the cheek, but nothing like the way he'd ravish me every other weekend.

The signs would become more apparent: loosestrife would invade their garden, dishes would remain piled dirty in the sink, unattended for days, and termites would slowly tear down the walls of the house.

Their intimacy would become perfunctory—a shared drink before bedtime, maybe a little conversation. Gestures would replace speech.

They'd forget the color of each other's eyes since it would have been so long since they'd held a gaze.

Then that day would come when they'd clasp each other's hands across a table and know the final curtain had descended and they must bow out. But gracefully.

Though tonight, LeShaun's absence was a cold embrace that sent me back inside.

The bottle of wine now floated in melting ice.

The last CD was on its last song.

I thought maybe he'd been delayed and would arrive in the morning.

I turned the oven off, where the food had been keeping warm, and started for bed.

I got halfway down the hall before I remembered to blow out the candles.

I stood at the dining room table confused before I realized I hadn't lit them in the first place.

Part III

SOME OF US ARE GENETICALLY PREDISPOSED

Our lives tremble

between pathos and seduction.

Our inhibitions

force us to be equal.

We swallow hard

black love potions

from a golden glass.

—Essex Hemphill

"Between Pathos and Seduction"

Dearest Darky

There are a few blackfolk who are servers when you start in the restaurant business in 2001 but only one who is a bartender. The other blackfolk, when there are any, usually work as dishwashers, and only a handful get to grill or bake.

You're trained by whitefolk who tell you that if you want to make bank as a server, you must follow simple protocols:

When listing the daily specials, state the most expensive items last since these are usually the items guests are most likely to remember. This will increase the odds that they'll order them.

Take orders in the following sequence: ladies first, oldest to youngest, followed by men, oldest to youngest; though, when you place the order with the kitchen, do so in the order that the guests are seated at the table, not the order in which you took it. This will prevent the wrong person from receiving the wrong entrée should someone else run your food.

If there are children, ask whether they should be served immediately while everyone else enjoys their soup and salad.

Bring the soup first, before the salad. Be sure to ask which salad: Caesar, house, or wedge. Don't forget the avocado ranch dressing comes on the wedge with blue cheese *crumbles*; this can be confusing for guests if not clarified. All the dressings are *house-made*. Specify those that are the house favorites.

When serving hot soup, pay close attention to guests who swing wide with their arms; remove the soup bowls before serving the salads.

When serving guests who are sitting in a booth, serve with your right hand if serving the left side of the booth, and the left hand if serving the right side. You should give the appearance of a hug instead of a backhanded slap (which is what will happen if the wrong hand is used on the wrong side of the booth).

If the restaurant is extremely busy and the kitchen is backed up, place the entrée orders before bringing the soup or salad.

When a guest makes a request, never respond with, *No problem*; this implies there is a problem. *Yes, ma'am* or *Yes, sir* is always appropriate.

Never take orders from children.

You will be employed by the Copper Cellar family of restaurants, which is based in your hometown of Knoxville, Tennessee. You will wait tables at Calhoun's, which is famous for having won the title of Best Ribs in America in 1983.

You will work there, at the White Bridge Road location in Nashville, while you're a student at Tennessee State University, but when you transfer to the University of Tennessee, you will transfer to the Calhoun's on Bearden Hill in Knoxville.

You will have risen in the ranks by this time, not least of all due to your uniform being deemed the best nearly every shift because you take the time to press your khaki pants and your blue-striped dress shirt, and you ensure your white apron has a sharp crease down the center.

Your white guests will often joke that you could cut someone with that crease. Sometimes you want to.

You wait on a grandfather having lunch with his granddaughter, and after you've delivered their food, he asks to see your hand. When you show him your hand, he grabs it and begins to rub it gently, marveling to his granddaughter: See how smooth the brown skin is? She buries her face in her hands, shaking her head in shock, and when she finally looks up, mouth agape, you ask if there's anything else you can do for them and leave her to stare at her grandfather while he eats his fried catfish and coleslaw, exclaiming how they are the most perfect combination.

You work the lunch shifts so you'll be guaranteed the prime sections on nights and weekends. You average three a week but try to avoid doubles as much as possible.

You are admired for being a team player, performing bathroom checks when asked, decrumbing the cracks in the booths, sweeping the cigarette butts from the parking lot.

You run food to a table of six, a table that isn't yours. After you've made sure no one needs anything further, you head to the kitchen to return the serving tray. You are unaware the server for whom you've just run food has been looking for you. When she finds you, she approaches you, waving a long white strip of paper in her hand, and tells you that one of the ladies from her table had flagged her down to give it to her. You notice she is holding the order ticket (or chit) you used to deliver the food. The sever says the lady at the table, as if in a panic, called out to her—Miss! Miss!—over the chatter in the restaurant, and beckoned her closer to the table to tell her, That colored boy dropped this ticket.

The server, who is white, laughs because she can't believe in 2001 that white ladies are still using *colored* to identify black people.

You laugh because you can't believe the lady tracked the server down to give her the chit. You crumple it and attempt to toss it into the trash can but miss. You watch it bounce off the rim onto the floor and think to yourself how you've never been good at basketball.

You will work for almost two years at Calhoun's before you are poached by the managers of the Copper Cellar, the corporation's flagship restaurant, to work there.

You want to work there because it is on the Strip, the main drag on the University of Tennessee campus, and during football season, you have heard that servers and bartenders have been known to make two months' rent in a single weekend. The added bonus is that your dorm is within walking distance.

You will work at the Copper Cellar off and on for seven years.

In your final stint working there, you will return to the restaurant broke at twenty-eight years old, having lost two serving jobs in Austin, Texas, each of them because you were either caught drinking on the job or you called in one time too many. Luckily, the same guests who'd become your benefactors over the years are still there when you return. They are old white couples who have tipped you into the thousands of dollars for your service, in addition to gifting you with Christmas and birthday bonuses. Some have paid all your expenses to the casino in Tunica, Mississippi—including money to gamble with—while others have insisted you bring a plate to the table and share large portions of their meals.

A few of the women love to claim to be your second mother; they've even invited your mama to dinner and told her the same. You are their family, their favorite, their baby boy, although the one most insistent on this fact is the one who makes kissy faces at you as she pinches your cheeks and calls you her dearest darky.

You consider leaving the Copper Cellar after you catch several of your white female coworkers in the banquet room, which is adjacent to the main dining room, with the lights dimmed just low enough for them to see each other's faces while they hatch a plan against you in angry whispers. They elect a whitegirl who wants to be a cop and who has wide hips and what she says is a blackgirl booty to be their leader. She accuses you of sharking all the good tables, and she says the girls intend to do something about it.

You make the decision to leave the Copper Cellar one afternoon when you're with a former coworker, having an early dinner at Chesapeake's, the corporation's premier seafood house. You tell her about the coup against you and listen to her scoff at the nerve of, as she calls them, those white bitches. And because she too is white, you take her rebuke as objectivity, which makes you feel better. It's during this exchange that the general manager—whom you worked with at Calhoun's on Bearden Hill and again when he hired you back at the Copper Cellar after your return from Texas—tells you that you're always welcome to come work for him at Chesapeake's whenever you want.

Two weeks later, you start orientation there.

Two years after that, you are promoted to bartender.

What you love about bartending is that the service is straightforward. You make drinks on request. You collect payments. You throw tips in a jar.

How much you make often depends on the merits of a cocktail. If you make it right, it should loosen a patron's inhibitions but not their resolve. It should be agreeable to the palate. Even if it's high in proof—or has an alcohol content of 50 percent or more—a cocktail should have a pleasant mouth feel.

You once make a cocktail for a lady dining in the lounge, a perfect Manhattan, equal parts dry and sweet vermouth, Angostura bitters, and Woodford Reserve served on the rocks with a maraschino cherry to garnish. After a few sips, she makes eye contact and lifts her glass: Cheers! Before she leaves, she approaches the bar, takes your hand firmly, and shakes it as she places five dollars in your palm.

You have bar guests whom you rely on for tips, but when there are guests dining at tables, tipping you randomly—and this happens to you often—then you're making money.

On the other hand, when business is sluggish, you entertain yourself by popping beer bottle caps into a trash can nearby, perusing recipes on Pinterest, stalking the restaurant until you find that a cadre of Scarlett O'Haras dependent upon the kindness of strangers has given up on the possibility of making any money and decided to get a jump on their side work, polishing and rolling silverware.

You bitch to them about how much money you need to pay this bill or that bill, and how sad it is that dinner means nibbling on a piece of bread dipped in drawn butter because you're too broke to afford anything more substantial to eat— even with the 40 percent employee discount.

Except you've been known to meet an income quota by the thinnest margins. The trick is to observe one rule of thumb: charisma is as important as pouring a good drink.

You try always to encourage a convivial atmosphere for guests who choose your services.

Your attitude invites them to step up to the bar, and you will wipe a clean spot cleaner just to show them you care.

When you slide a beverage napkin their way, you let them know you're listening.

The dining room guests can have their tables and captain's chairs—at the bar, everyone shares the throne.

May I suggest the filet mignon and cold-water lobster tails this evening? you might say. But first you will insist that they consider a menu of six-dollar appetizers while you woo them with offers of two bucks off wine by the glass and liquor by the drink, half off draft beer, a dollar off bottled. These are the happy hour specials (when generous pours can be exchanged for hefty tips, and this—your mutually agreed upon quid pro quo—can be initiated with a wink and a nod, a fist bump or thumbs-up).

Of course, there's always that one guest, usually a regular, who, no matter what, will leave a pittance for a tip.

One in particular demands that you wash and polish a snifter for him to slosh his cheap bourbon.

He's fond of telling everyone that he might not always be right, but he's never wrong, and the future just ain't what it used to be.

You don't want to encourage him to expose the wounds of his failing marriage, or else he is likely to grab the crook of your arm when you try to walk away from him because he needs you to listen for just a minute because he has something very important to tell you about marriage, and you have to know it this very instant or else your life will be damaged beyond repair. He makes you bend low—so low his hand rests on your shoulder, so low he breathes his whiskey breath into your face—because you must know this, he says, and you'll thank him later for informing you that despite what you've been told in the past by your mother or father or your wife, it just isn't true that when you're slicing vegetables and accidentally drop a knife, you should simply let it fall to the floor. You try to catch it! Don't let utensils hit the floor with all that filth. Just mind the blade!

He tells you this, and you shake your head and say, Yes, sir, but you think, *Why, Lord?* Because you know you're going to get a paltry tip, but still you must provide him the kindest service. You can pat him on the hand still clenched firmly around your arm, tell him that you will remember, and thank him for looking out for you.

You will often make the best money off a group of regulars who are white men from the surrounding boondock counties who make sure that you always keep a drink in their hands. You will observe as they grow gradually drunker and drunker, and you'll slow down the service, but you won't cut them off. You'll stay blasé when they slur, when they sit half-tilted off their stools, when their voices boom with boisterous laughter, or when they lean in with a hushed tone to sneak a few *niggers* into their sentences because you know they're not racist, they tell you. You know I love you, brother! they say.

In fact, one of these white men has a wonderful joke, you think, about a particular type of nigger, a joke that you'll repeat yourself.

It's the joke about a white couple, John and Wendy, who get married in a lavish ceremony. John loves Wendy very much, and as his promise of fidelity, he has her name tattooed on his penis. For their honeymoon, they travel to Jamaica, and every night, Wendy is tickled when the *WY* on his flaccid penis expands into her full name when John gets erect. One night at a bar, John tries a variety of delicious rum drinks, which causes him to piss frequently. On one of his trips to the men's room, he takes a urinal next to a gentleman who appears to be a local. Curious—as some men are in these situations—John peeks over at the local to discover he has the letters *WY* tattooed on his penis as well. What a coincidence, he thinks. Excuse me, John says when they're each washing their hands at the sink. I noticed that you have *WY* tattooed on your penis. I do too! It stands for Wendy, my beautiful wife. We're here on our honeymoon. What does your *WY* stand for? The local turns to John with equal enthusiasm and says, well, *WY* does not stand for Wendy. He pauses a moment to toss his paper towel into the trash bin. It stands for Welcome to Jamaica, Have a Nice Day!

When you tell this joke to bar guests whom you feel you can trust, much like the white man from whom you learned the joke, you will whisper it to them because it's a pretty raucous dick joke that needs to be told discreetly but not at all because you believe it's racist.

It's only a joke, and you don't want to acknowledge the implied history of racialized terror against black men when white men thought about the size of a black man's dick.

You chalk it up to a joke about penis envy and not about what white men fear a black man's dick would do to their white women.

Racial politics have no place in how you pay your bills, even though when you recall your experiences working at the various Copper Cellar family of restaurants, you will tell folks, incredulously, about *See how smooth the brown skin is?* and *Miss, that colored boy dropped this ticket,* and *Hey there, my dearest darky,* and the joke about John and Wendy.

You will tell folks how you couldn't have made the money you did without managers who gave you prime schedules, and that you took a pay cut when you went off to graduate school.

You will tell folks about the time a manager told you to smile so everyone could see your teeth and identify you in the dark when the lights went out in the restaurant during a power failure, or the time another manager called you a niglet for reasons you still can't fathom.

You won't tell folks how you often complained alongside your white coworkers about hating to wait on blackfolk because blackfolk don't tip.

You won't tell folks how you were largely responsible for getting a whitegirl fired for refusing to wait on a table of blackfolk because it was the only way you could get her fired because you didn't like her.

You won't tell folks you didn't like her because she made overtly sexual comments just like everyone else, but unlike everyone else, she was obese, and you were fatphobic, and many of your coworkers urged you to play the race card against her to get her fired since this would be the only way to get rid of her.

You won't tell folks there were many strategies you used to prevent otherwise excellent servers from getting better shifts than you.

You won't tell folks what you fear any of this says about you, what it might have to do with how you want people to feel about you, which is that you've always wanted people to like you, that you don't know the limits you'll go to to make sure that people will always like you, and you can't see how there's anything wrong with that.

Imaginary Friend

All your work friends believe you like to drink alone so that you can drink too much.

It's true, but you hate that they know it.

So you invent a buddy named Darnell.

Whenever your friends ask you to go out for drinks after work, you'll go sometimes, but those times when you don't really want to, especially when you're trying to save money, you tell them you and Darnell have already arranged to have drinks.

Bring him with you, they'll say.

He's having a bad day, you'll say. Maybe next time.

They'll roll their eyes because when it comes to Darnell, next time never comes. But no matter, no one ever knows you're really at home on your porch, deliriously shit-faced, shouting, with each drink, Go with bourbon, pal, one ice cube.

This is how you play the sophisticated cheat and lessen the guilt of drinking alone.

You tell yourself:

Think chameleon trickery.

Act the part from the roots of your hair down to your cuticles.

Create a backstory you believe in.

You read an article once that says poets have the highest mortality rate of all writers, most likely because they *partook* too much. This is perfect. You have a Master of Fine Arts, so it's quite easy for you to become poet-as-consummate-boozehound, the life of your own party.

Consecrate the role, you tell yourself. *Versify your speech.*

If someone asks if you'd like a glass of wine, you should respond with a quote from Sexton or Plath or Berryman or Crane. It don't even have to make sense. Just go with it. They'll think you're a douche. So let them. Be the douche, you say. The key to sophistication is to own it.

Consider setting. Interior: a radio turned low, a slow circling fan brandishing its shadows on the ceiling, a lone bare bulb in a shaded room, sheer silk scarves draped across the radiator, cigarette smoke courting spliced light through the blinds. Curl on the sofa, limp arm dangling across a tattered armrest, grasping a bottle in hand.

Absolutely photogenic.

These visuals prove that yes, you are indeed pathetic if not also a cliché, which is just the right amount of pathos you need to pull this off. And when, undoubtedly, your friends continue to invite you out for drinks, you have to stay the course. You've forgotten that, often, they extend these invitations when they're just as drunk themselves. Just saying no won't cut it.

You've told them you can no longer carouse around bars, in dives, with all those drunken strangers spoiling the fermentation: buzzkillers toking cheap swag, toe-steppers, back-shovers, table-bumpers—no adulation there—not to mention beer-spillers, vomit-spewers, and fake ID loudmouths who won't shut the fuck up.

You want to be alone, you say.

You work each night, counting down the hours until you can go home by yourself, anxious that you've had to wait until after you've swept up the last piles of dust, dumped them among the rest of the junk; after you've filled the grinders with pepper, the salt shakers, the artificial sweeteners; after you've tightened the rolls of silverware in their blue linen suits, lined them four in a row on each table like bodies dead on a battlefield. After the busiest nights too often spent at war with grime the most feverish scrubbing can't uncake from behind the silver tables sloshed with silverware sludge, buckets of grunge smeared like an avant-garde painting, so much filth clinging to each apparatus it becomes unbearable unless you remain vigilant and remember what awaits you, the gift that will arrive the quicker midnight approaches, when the aquarium lights are switched off, the bar left to glow semidark in neon blue fluorescence, the copper and brass paneling polished to a new-penny sheen.

Only then can you finally leave, startled by the hum of the workplace softened to a single thrummed string diminishing to white noise, the sound of water wrinkling when a lobster flips its tail swimming to the surface, then flits away as though it intends to secure in the darkened tank a nook to try its luck against hands it knows will eventually come reaching through the bitter cold water to gather it up and carry it forever away.

The Drunken Story

We're all here, me and a bunch of whiteboys . . . six or seven or maybe eight . . . I'm not sure I'm counting myself.

It's spring or fall, I don't remember which week. But it's so cold it could be either season—you know, when it's hard to tell when to wear a sweater or keep a box of condoms handy in case the rain gets a little chilly blowing off the river where the house tilts the hill above it . . .

At any rate, we're living off the gold digger, out in the front yard . . . all of us . . . and he says, Watch this, and he cuts a cue ball of cocaine in that *slice-swish-slice-swish* motion . . . you know . . . the seesaw amazed us all . . . such sleight of heel, our eyelashes singing.

Then he hands me a beer and I eat it fast, I'm so thirsty . . . liquid gushing like scum down the drain. I should be asleep . . .

it's two in the morning … it's four in the morning … hot …
the moon searing us like steaks in a Bundt pan.

But I have to be here with all these tramps, cocaine
tasting … back and forth the blade cutting the row of dynamite.
And it's a total, Dude! We're having a blast!

He whips off a rolled hundred-dollar bill … a straw cut
halfways … he plants his face against the glass, and ghosts
begin to disappear. He passes me the mirror, and I take a drag
from my cigarette, turn it upside down until the flashlight
glows like an ember … it's so beautiful I have to greet everyone!

I snort my line … but whiteboy must've gotten the last
because I feel nothing except hot coal in my nose.

But I don't care … we're skiing Mt. Olympics! And it's
the most tranquilizers I've ever felt.

He agrees. He gives me a shot of Jack Daniels since he
hears I'm from Tennessee, so I tell whiteboy, You're the only
ten I see, and kiss him hard …

Retrograde

My daddy finds a lump on the side of his neck and asks me, What do you think it is?

He sits down beside me on the couch, where I'm holding my sister's new baby in my lap, and takes my hand, presses two fingers against the hard nodule. He wants me to read the raised bump as if it were Braille, so that I might tell him what it is or isn't.

I'm not scared to die, he says and takes the baby from me.

He rises with her to his feet, unsteady, his legs wobbly.

We all have our time, he says to me, to the baby.

He holds her outstretched in front of him, then brings her in to nuzzle her belly, nibble her tiny hands.

We all have to go, he says and presses his nose to hers.

I watch him raise her high into the air, just below the slow turning blades of the ceiling fan, as if she were a goddess or an offering.

She gurgles and drools onto his face from above, the blades gently whipping the air against the back of her neck.

I get up from the couch and take the baby from him.

It's probably just a hair bump, I say.

Nah, he says and swats a hand at me.

He shuffles out of the room and into the kitchen.

I hear ice clinking into a glass, liquid pouring over the ice, the ice cracking.

He returns with his drink and sits in a chair.

For a while neither of us speaks.

Then he raises the glass as if to take a sip.

He pauses.

I know what a hair bump is, he says and takes a long swallow.

Some of Us
Are Genetically
Predisposed

E ight o'clock in the morning, without fail, the subtle
tremors would begin in my toes.

I'd try holding myself still to neutralize them, but
they resisted restraint, determined to turn violent if I didn't
allow them to take their course.

They'd travel north to visit the more sensitive parts of my
body—my earlobes, the tip of my nose, my eyelids.

They were erratic, plunging sharply south to my groin for
a pit stop before zipping north again to the crown of my head,
where they'd settle like a pot of simmering water.

My brain became a prickly kiwi sending communications
to the rest of my body along ropes of twine.

I was shot through with pins all over. Mostly, I needed to scratch.

I needed a drink, my body warned me, and not hair of the dog since I wasn't hungover, but a drink, and not just any drink, but the one that brought back my soul.

If only someone would've been there with me with a good bedside manner. Someone to fetch me cold compresses when my temperature rose to slightly above normal, when I felt my skin dampen. Someone to calm my body, to assure me that what I was experiencing wasn't a slow demise.

But there was no one. Only me, alone with my tremors.

Each day I tried to avoid drinking too early in the morning.

I eased out from underneath the hot sheets to stand naked by the side of the bed to let the cold air hit me. Only barely did this help to subdue the buzzing I felt at the edges of my skin.

I dragged my backside along the cold bedroom walls all the way to the hall.

In the hallway, I pressed my chest along those cold walls until I entered the bathroom.

In the bathroom, I sat on the cold toilet lid to rest my back against the cold porcelain tank.

I hoped all that coldness would soothe me.

I remained there, waiting for the tremors to subside, biting my lip, glimpsing my fatigued face in the bathroom mirror. My watery eyes. My runny nose.

I imagined I was a house with the bathtubs left overflowing, water seeping through the floorboards, through the ceiling, thick cataracts of it trickling down the walls until what amounted to pools and pools of water destroyed the house's once good bones down to its very foundation.

I sat, tapping a rhythm against the floor as if I were a prisoner found guilty of a deliberate and hostile act of destruction and I was awaiting sentencing, the gavel hammering down the verdict, and the clang of the gates securing me inside a cell.

I realized I was guilty of and had been ensnared by the one tragic flaw that had befallen several generations of Stewart men.

But on one of those mornings when my mouth went dry, and I turned on the faucet to let cold water run into my cupped hand, and I drank the water, only to let it dribble mostly from my lips, I had to face it—I needed liquor, immediately.

So I climbed the stairs to the second level on legs flimsy as kite string.

I stored my poison beneath the sink in the kitchen. Though when I opened the cabinet doors, I found only empty plastic bottles.

No, they were dead soldiers lined in a row like headstones.

No, dominoes toppling in disarray as I scavenged for one that might contain at least a promising nip trapped in its corners, rewarding me with a taste to tide me over until I went to my bartending job.

Though I wasn't without other options. I could (1) make the twenty-minute walk, round-trip, to the liquor store (which opened at eight); or (2) take my chances at the possibility there'd be enough vodka from those near-empty bottles to drip into my mouth.

I chose option two and lined the bottles end to end on the countertop.

I snaked them into rows when I ran out of room lengthwise.

When I placed the last bottle in the last available space, next to a bread knife, suddenly, the heretofore unknown option three presented an opportunity for ingenuity: if I used the knife to cut closer to the base of each bottle, forming a lip where the liquor could rest just shy of the considerably lowered brim, I could pour out more liquor.

Minding my fingers, I enacted the plan and managed to salvage more than a double shot of vodka. My tongue savored it eagerly before I swallowed it warm down my throat.

My muscles relaxed.

Content with newfound energy.

Nimble as I descended the stairs to the bedroom to get dressed for work.

I pulled on my pants quickly. Buttoned and tucked in my shirt. Looped and fastened my belt. Affixed my necktie. But where were my shoes? I folded my bar apron and placed it inside my messenger bag or else I'd forget it.

Then I stopped.

A gleaming half-gallon bottle of vodka prevented me from placing the apron neatly at the bottom of the bag.

I pulled it out and pressed it to my chest, hearing its *glug glug* sing so sweetly I almost began to harmonize with it.

I cracked the seal, removed the cap, and chugged hard.

It was surprisingly chilled.

I gulped again and again until I could hold the bottle steady, until my outstretched hand remained parallel to the floor without the slightest tremor.

My mission was accomplished. But now I was running late.

I slipped on my shoes, which had been hiding beneath the bed. Slung the messenger bag over my shoulder. Pet the dog goodbye. Dashed out the door and down the backyard hill to catch the bus.

As I ran, the bottle banged a bruise against my hipbone. I made it to the bus stop just in time. I reached inside the bag, tempted, as cars passed by one after another, to steal a long sip.

But I waited.

Nothing protected me from being seen on the corner tilting a half-gallon bottle to my lips at nine thirty in the morning.

Instead, I put my hand inside my bag and ran fingers across the bottle's embossed lettering until I could see the shape of the bus rounding a curve in the distance.

I counted a dollar and fifty cents in quarters into my hand when the bus pulled to the curb. I was humming *soon and very soon*, an old hymn I learned as a child in church when the congregation sang prayers of thanks and contrition. I boarded and paid the fare, still humming, a little softer now, as I walked past passengers with tired faces to an empty seat at the back, feeling the liquor's weight shifting inside the bottle.

Part IV

PATIENT ZERO

I struggle against
plagues, plots,
pressure,
paranoia.
Everyone wants a price
for my living.

—Essex Hemphill
"The Tomb of Sorrow"

Revelations

I was visiting family over winter break from the University of Tennessee and made sure to stop in at my old job, Calhoun's on White Bridge Road. I was hankering to see my old coworkers, my old friends, and to gobble up a platter of BBQ baby back ribs and fried catfish. I went there on Sunday, December 16, a date memorable for two events, one of which I can't entirely recall.

When I arrived, the restaurant was emptying gradually, the majority of tables vacant, a few guests straggling at the bar, and only the closers were waiting out the final minutes before the doors could be locked. On the second level, a few servers rolled silverware. After finishing my meal, I helped them with their side work while nursing a last-minute cocktail—double vodka and cranberry, perhaps, or maybe a beer, or a martini on the rocks—until someone bounded up the stairs to tell us that an Olympic torch carrier would soon pass by the restaurant on the way to Louisville, Kentucky, en route to Salt Lake City, Utah, for the 2002 Winter Olympic Games. And so we all clamored outdoors into the Sunday evening drizzle. The street glistening from the soft rain, barely visible if not for headlights of passing cars. Or maybe there was no glisten, and it wasn't raining, and perhaps my eyes were gilded over from too many pints of Helles, my favorite craft lager, or from the Irish car bombs I settled on for dessert, or the drink I nursed after that, which is why I misremember this particular detail about the weather and also whether it was a man or a woman carrying the torch, their caravan including a news team and flashing lights following closely behind. Why it's important that I remember, I'm not sure, except that night was a once-in-a-lifetime opportunity to witness the fiftieth anniversary of the Winter Olympic torch relay.

But what I do remember clearly, after the cheering and the national pride that had welled inside us subsided—I asked one of my server friends, Wallace or Willis, for a ride home. I remember he said yes, but that he had to pick up a friend first. And so we climbed into his truck to go get him.

As Wallace or Willis maneuvered out of the parking lot, he looked at me a few times as if there was something he needed to say but didn't know how. Furtive glances for five minutes, ten minutes, and then we were there at the friend's apartment. He was waiting outside for us. As the friend approached the truck, those furtive glances returned as if Wallace or Willis were running out of time, his mouth a trap door opening and closing tight, no sound, and then just as the door creaked open, before the friend eased himself into the cab beside me, Wallace or Willis whispered to me that his friend was HIV positive. I didn't understand what it was he had thought to do with this revelation. Warn me?

I had nothing to say. It was 2001, and I was twenty-two, which is important if you're to understand my perspective that people with HIV seemed only to exist in books and movies and on the eleven-o'clock news, not in Wallace or Willis's truck, not as a person whose name is babbled to initiate an introduction, this friend who climbed inside, brushing his arm against mine, compelling me, stuck in the middle, to scoot a little to my left. And when the friend made himself more comfortable within the tight space, the entire left side of his body pressed against the entire right side of mine, I thought about how this could not be happening to me. That surely our shoulders, forearms, thighs, calves were not all in close, intimate contact. And when I scooted even more to the left but couldn't get enough air between us, lamenting how I hadn't worn a long sleeve shirt—and why hadn't he?—surely it was rational that I prayed this man would not infect me.

I rode the rest of the way hunched in the middle, my body attempting to ball itself into a safe sphere. I thought it polite to mumble a greeting that seemed genuine yet that prepared him for my decision to engage him no more than necessary.

But what was I afraid of?

He looked *normal*. I had expected to find a man striving for composure the way a despondent man might with his mouth agape and drooling, eyes sunken as if his face intended to make a cave of its own flesh.

I expected to sit beside him while he moaned, as if some creation inside him was struggling to bear itself into the world, as if he were reincarnating himself, allowing himself a second chance to avoid mistakes made in his past life.

I expected him to calm himself so that when he returned to normal breathing, he would do so softly, so that I would feel the machinery of my inner ears churning to process if he were making any sounds at all.

I expected him to rest a bleached head on my shoulder and for me to hear the tide of his voice rolling in and out, mumbling on about four-leaf clovers and other superstitions, the result of the toll the virus had taken on his body.

I expected to push him away against the window, to shudder when I heard his head knocking against the pane of glass.

Except he was nothing like in my imagination.

His healthy head of jet black, shoulder-length hair made his fair skin appear paler than it probably was, especially in that evening's light, when even that could make him resemble nothing of the sick and shut-in, the plagued.

He was something of a waif. But so was Wallace or Willis.

Yet still I rode the rest of the way, sitting on my clenched hands, taking in sips of air, my face tilted toward the driver's side.

Was I grateful that when Wallace or Willis dropped me off, his friend gave me a wide berth?

Perhaps not. Perhaps I was merely relieved that we spent the entire ride in silence, and no one said a word to break it.

How to Reconcile

There's so much I have to tell you, Jerome said.

It had been nearly two years since we'd seen one another, and we'd finally found time to reconnect at Atlanta Pride in 2003.

We'd been driving around downtown the way we used to do in Nashville, in the early college years when we were still in the twentieth century. But instead of the usual raucous shenanigans we incited in one another, he turned down the volume on the radio, rolled up the windows so the wind wouldn't whip so loudly.

He became a different Jerome from the one who, not even an hour earlier, had been serving disappointment to all of the black gay boys in Piedmont Park who weren't quite giving it the best that they got, he'd said, channeling Anita Baker, referring to how many of them performed their runway walks and J-Sette routines to lackluster effect. Now, as he pulled into an empty parking space, he grew somber, stilled.

I sensed we wouldn't sit in that car continuing to fall into that familiar rhythm best friends seem never to lose even after years without a word passing between them. This wasn't going to be an occasion for plebeian pleasantries, no *how you beens* or *been too longs* or the unremarkable small talk that required no context.

And so I prepared myself as best I could, noticing the clouds stretched like fabric in the cobalt sky, which blinked with planes taking off or landing, the tall buildings teetering their bright heads toward Orion's Belt, the absent stars.

I'm positive, he said swiftly, without ceremony. As if this wasn't a confession, an unburdening—just a fact.

My breath caught in my throat at the revelation's bluntness, the force of nonchalance thinning the air the way I presumed it did when one ascended a steep mountain or contemplated entering an ocean threatening to roil.

I felt the appropriate reaction would be to cry. But I couldn't.

Only a few weeks before, I'd watched *Forrest Gump*, drunk on a pint of vodka. I'd wept like a fool at the piano solo during the end credits, right before the moaning ghosts begin to sing. The melody played in my head as I tried my best to bring water to well in my eyes.

Did you hear me? he said.

I just shook my head. What else was there to say?

I meant to say, yes, I heard you.

He told me about the night he got his cakes beat up at Houston Splash (another of the black Pride destinations), his body pressed up against the window of a Holiday Inn overlooking the parking lot. He wasn't using protection, and when the dude came inside him, Jerome said he knew right then he'd been infected.

But how could you know? I said.

Chile, I was a patented whore, he said. It was only a matter of time.

I hadn't seen Jerome in almost two years, so I thought it rude of me not to conjure from all the lost months, weeks, days, hours, minutes some semblance of grief to display. But I knew this would be contrived, and I was too self-conscious, believing I'd failed to articulate the proper amount of empathy. I didn't want him to mistake my reaction—or lack thereof—for judgment.

All I could muster was a crack in my voice.

It's okay if you want to cry, he said, and though I did feel my eyes become wet, it was likely due to me needing to yawn. It was getting late. I was tired.

I'm gonna be okay, he said. I'll be perfectly fine, dahling.

I detected not a trace of fear, of self-recrimination. Jerome was absolutely confident that his future would never be plagued by the specter of death.

Except it was.

Thirteen years is a long time, which is how long it took for him to die of full-blown AIDS.

And I couldn't understand how that was possible.

I called our friend Marshall, who I knew had kept in better contact with him. He told me that Jerome had become withdrawn, that he'd begun to drink heavily, to the point where he'd received at least a couple DUIs.

Jerome became more secretive over the years, moving from one city to another without notice, as though he were shedding himself in each one.

Jerome lied about routine medical procedures but particularly about his dental visits that were actually appointments to have Kaposi sarcoma lesions surgically removed from his mouth.

Jerome's apartment was a horde of pornography, condoms, lubricants, enema paraphernalia, and unopened bottles of antiretrovirals prescribed to him from the various cities he'd lived in—enough to construct a mural on his living room wall.

Jerome's medical records he'd left strewn across his apartment floors showed his T cell count at virtually zero.

Jerome's friends had to get rid of all this before his family arrived to claim his body.

Jerome's family wouldn't know his cause of death.

Jerome's family never knew he was HIV positive.

He'd taken it all to the grave, and the service celebrating his life carried on, reminiscent of the plague years, when many families refused to acknowledge the true cause of death that was never cancer, pneumonia, a heart attack, or the simply unknown.

For weeks after, I spun yarns around my heart, considering Jerome's future had he just taken the pills. If he could have just *managed* and not given up.

Was he, like me, afraid of loneliness, of being lulled to sleep with no body to warm him, no dent in the mattress to remind him he'd missed a thousand and more habitual nights of companionship?

If the days weren't so filled with the natural order of things—birds' quick-beat flapping when escaping danger, or the quieter tenor of fish leaping, flopping mid-air, resplendent in the river—I might have grown bitter, believing that surviving the dead was an act of unkindness.

Nodding politely to a woman carrying her child on her hip simply means the world indeed continues to revolve, the moon still cycles, and tides continue to excavate rubble and wash it ashore.

And I wouldn't have to search my memories of him that survived, for the characteristics that I would forever associate with him—like how he would sweat so easily no matter the temperature—and so I could just imagine him deliberately sunning himself on hot afternoons, hoping that if he perspired, the virus would flee his body like a flock of crows because his mission was to live.

I would like to remember Jerome like this, not with his possible fear of loneliness: the mattress worn smooth, the dishes collecting dust in the cabinet.

No, let my memories of him be the sun ravaging him with light, and those birds lost somewhere in his body's cast shadow.

Call Me When
You Get This

returned a phone call from a woman whose name I couldn't remember. I'd met her only a handful of times. What I remember most about her is that she was overly familiar, justifying her closeness by telling me how she'd known me since way back when.

She'd seen the cakes I'd baked and posted on Facebook, and she got my number from my boyfriend, Andre. She called me, but because I didn't answer phone calls from numbers I didn't recognize, she left a message asking if I would bake one for her.

I met her at Andre's house one afternoon a few days later. Her cake sat on the counter in the kitchen. She had brought a friend with her to pick it up, and the two of them sat at the table in the dining room. I placed the cake in the center of the table. They remarked how good it smelled, but I was eager for her to pay me and for the two of them to leave. But they didn't. And true to her nature, she couldn't leave just yet because she needed to pitch me an idea. She said that if I wanted to make more money, more than what I made baking cakes for folks—which hadn't been much at all—I needed to donate plasma.

I gave her no impression that I was interested in hearing this but nodded anyway just to be cordial. I'd heard this campaign before about donating plasma, so I muttered, mostly to myself, Yeah, sure.

And she said, No, really. They talk about it in those commercials, I see the ads on billboards and flyers at the grocery store all the time. They're trying to pay everybody for their blood.

She wouldn't let up. Her eyes were so wide and full of expressive assuredness they seemed almost to frolic, yet it made me wince a little, knowing that to get her to understand the full measure of my disinterest, I'd have to explain why I thought it might be impossible for me to donate plasma. I wasn't exactly sure why, but I had a feeling it wouldn't work out.

Though by this point, perhaps sensing how little I seemed to care, she gestured to the other woman sitting with us—next to me, in fact—whose name I didn't catch. The other woman agreed and told me in the same frantic way about the great opportunity to donate plasma.

Eventually, it became clear to them both that I didn't want to hear any more about it. Perhaps from the look on my face, they sensed that something more was going on and that they might have overstepped.

I wanted to cut them some slack. It wasn't as if I'd already told them why I was afraid to donate plasma and they'd forgotten. This came as some relief. I wouldn't have felt comfortable explaining the reason to them, staring into their eyes the way, supposedly, someone like me might do to say tacitly, *Please don't make me say it out loud*. This way, they wouldn't grow so quiet, the first time all afternoon, and sit there stricken with their sad brown eyes brimming wet with the threat of tears. They wouldn't be forced to look across the table to one another and, like sisters in all this, feel overly apologetic because they'd attempted to convince me to donate plasma, not understanding how frightened I was of what I might learn about myself, that if I went ahead with it, I'd most certainly receive a call one day from an unknown number and let it go to voicemail so that I could delay a little longer the revelation that someone had left a message for me to return a call so they could thank me for donating plasma but that they were afraid, and they were sorry, my blood wasn't viable, not safe, not clean.

Patient Zero

was born a blackboy in Knoxville, Tennessee, in 1979, when many gay blackboys believed the arrival of a mysterious gay cancer in the early eighties was strictly a gay whiteboy's disease. The white media had them convinced that a whiteboy from Quebec City, Quebec, an airline steward who spent considerable time relishing the spoils of the world—particularly the coastal hubs of gay sex life in San Francisco and New York—had brought AIDS to the United States.

Though he was identified anonymously as *Patient O*— the letter *O* meaning *Out of California*—and then mistaken for *Patient 0* because that's what happens when you can't tell an *O* from a zero, he was finally identified as *Patient Zero*, and the man who would be seldom known to the world by his given name, Gaëtan Dugas, became the antihero of the AIDS saga.

Though how was it possible that a single whiteboy could bring a fatal virus into the United States?

Medical scientists found in Dugas's address book what they believed to be the answer. They learned that Dugas had had sex with the men listed in that book. They learned that those men then had sex with other men, and then learned that those men then had sex with other men.

And then other men.

And more and more men traced back to Dugas were having sex.

Many of those men, as a result, had become mysteriously ill from a virus that medical scientists at the time termed GRID, or Gay-Related Immune Deficiency.

But when confronted with this information, sources claimed Dugas didn't accept that he had a communicable disease, let alone GRID, even when he showed symptoms similar to those of his infected sex partners. Instead, one of the symptoms—a purple lesion behind his ear that was subsequently cut off and biopsied—was revealed by his doctor to be Kaposi sarcoma, a type of skin cancer. So Dugas believed he had cancer. And cancer couldn't be transmitted sexually. So Dugas continued to fuck as he always had, claiming to have had 2,500 sexual partners over a ten-year period—250 lays a year—even when doctors implored him not to. He even refused to wear a condom.

So Dugas, according to myth, continued to enter crowded discos, surveying the compacted bodies while exclaiming to himself and to all, I am the prettiest one, and he made his way among the throng while denying that he carried inside him a malignancy that would reduce all that glitter to dust.

And the hundreds of men who believed he was the prettiest one—they would bed him again and again.

By the time Dugas died in 1984 from complications due to AIDS, he would do so amid rumors that in the cubicles of those bathhouses and sex bars, he would dim the lights dimmer so his accumulating lesions would not show the effects of the disease he swore was cancer, insisting upon having a body lie there with a can of Crisco and a bottle of poppers so that he might luxuriate in the looming conquest.

And when the sex was over, Dugas would brighten the lights to point out the lesions to his partners and say to them, I've got gay cancer . . . I'm going to die, and so are you.

But Gaëtan Dugas, we know now, was not Patient Zero but somebody to blame.

Nevertheless, as I was coming of age, and as far as those blackboys who were having sex with other blackboys knew, the men Dugas infected were all white, and that meant something.

Weren't whiteboys, for so long, the poster children for AIDS?

It was no wonder those blackboys believed *I won't catch it. I can't catch it.*

And by the time I became sexually active in the late nineties, I was fucking other blackboys who believed the same. By the early to mid-2000s, I'd gone buck wild.

I tried crack for the first time, then gave it up for cocaine.

I used cocaine to seduce straight boys at parties from twilight to sunup.

I seduced the straight boys with bottles of wine and dinners for two, pretending to have the kind of relationship that couldn't last.

I gave up pursuing the straight boys and instead went for the sure thing, one-night stands with as many men as I could meet in bars but especially those who hid behind computer screens, scouring my numerous online profiles, sending chat-room friend requests—all of us wanting more drugs, more liquor, more sex to fulfill the thrill of being reckless.

Gradually, these one-night stands became a feast of whiteboys.

Whiteboys whose profile tags read: BLACK COCK TO THE FRONT OF THE LINE.

Whiteboys who sent messages with pictures of their assholes, begging to be plowed and cream-pied. Whiteboys for whom I was the satiation of a dream.

Whiteboys who made it impossible for me to realize how close I was to becoming yet another infected blackboy tipping the balance so that HIV became less and less a whiteboy's disease.

Whiteboys whom I might one day be looking for.

Whiteboys who might one day be looking for me.

Whiteboys

'm trying to remember who you are again.

Some of you, anyway.

We were living in Austin. I was a graduate student at the University of Texas, and you were all a familiar face

at Halcyon

or Charley's

or Oilcan Harry's

or Rain

or Elysium

or Red Fez

or Dive Bar

or Crown and Anchor

or Dog and Duck

or Opal Divine's

or Raggedy Anne's.

I'd gone through a phase of hooking up with whiteboys, even though I said I would *never* hook up with whiteboys.

Pinkies, my best friend, Jerome, used to call them.

Of course, I said *I'd never* about many things: drinking liquor harder than white zinfandel, or a cocktail that wasn't meant to be served in a hurricane glass with an umbrella.

I'd never smoke cigarettes

or crack

or snort cocaine

or trip on ecstasy

or mushrooms.

And you were my very first whiteboy. We met at a party at the home of mutual friends. You found me alone in their backyard at a picnic table, drinking vodka with a splash of cranberry (to give it color), smoking a cigarette as I cut lines of coke on a plate I'd taken from the kitchen cabinet.

I didn't hear you approaching from behind, nor did I know if you noticed how often I ducked beneath the table, looking for a rolled-up five-dollar bill that kept falling to the ground.

Maybe you noticed me place it in the grooves of the ashtray to hold it still while I finished cutting the lines.

Maybe you found it odd when I took a drag off the cigarette and placed it in the ashtray, but instead of the rolled-up bill, I picked up the cigarette again. I turned it around as if admiring the smoldering ember. I bent over the plate with it and tried to snort a line through its lit end.

But if you'd seen what happened, you said nothing about how fucked up I must have already been.

I flinched in pain, and I think you confused it for something else.

You said you were sorry if you startled me.

I relaxed because you said *startled*. I asked you to sit with me. I explained how I'd burned my nose on the cigarette, and you said you'd be right back. And you were, with ice cubes wrapped in a bright blue rag. You held it to my nose.

I asked if you were trying to get my draws.

You were a whiteboy who said *startled*, so you didn't get my reference.

I offered you a line, and you took the plate. I passed you my flask, and you took a quick swig. You usually drank Southern Comfort, you said.

You said you weren't completely straight.

This was how we got to know one another, sharing a plate of cocaine and a flask of vodka.

Later, when the party migrated to the gay bars on Fourth Street, I got to see what you meant by *not completely straight*. I took you into an oversized porta-potty in the back courtyard of one of those bars.

You peered through the door just as it closed as if to make sure no one saw you go in with me.

When we were safely inside, a motion-sensor light dimly lit your face. You may have been considering that you'd made a mistake. Were you ready?

Not that it mattered to me.

I stuck my hand down your pants and breathed into your neck. I pulled the elastic waistband of your boxers.

These are your draws, I said.

Let's get out of here, you said.

We took a cab back to the party house, where you said you were staying the night.

We finished the rest of the cocaine.

We drank the beer left in the refrigerator.

You told me you were a Scorpio.

I asked you if Scorpios really were the best.

We sucked each other off.

You said it was your first time.

I laughed and said, Not mine.

You came.

I didn't.

I stayed the night as well, and in the morning, you weren't in bed with me when I woke up. As I dressed, I found a note you'd passed beneath the bedroom door, asking me to keep our hookup to myself. I later texted you I would.

I didn't keep that promise.

I told my housemates you had a square dick and that you came in my mouth without warning me first.

The disrespect! my housemates said.

At another party, high on cocaine, I told a crowd of my friends the same thing.

Whoever heard of a square dick? they said.

I still hoped I could see you more after that night, that maybe we could become better acquaintances, friends, fuck buddies.

I saw you only once in a while, though. We never spoke. I'd wave, but you wouldn't wave back.

I wondered if it had gotten back to you that I'd talked about your square dick, that I'd broken my promise to keep our hookup a secret.

I could tell you it was a moment of weakness, that I was only trying to get a laugh, that something insecure in me had reared itself up in front of a crowd I entertained at your expense.

I could say that I was sorry, that I was petty, that I'd always been.

I could offer a small consolation. I still have a small black dot on the tip of my nose from that cigarette burn. The best it will ever heal.

———

You were a married whiteboy.

Your wife brought you to Charley's on your birthday. We drank vodka cranberries, which is what prompted your wife to chat. She found our common tastes in cocktails to be alluring, I suppose.

She had a purpose, though. She was looking to find a boy willing to suck your cock. Because I'm not good at it, she whispered. She had a slight lisp that I imagined had grown more subdued from her sorority days at the university.

It's also the way she said *cock*. As if she'd heard the word spoken only in the porn the two of you watched once in a while when you were feeling adventurous. Like that night.

It's the way you let her do most of the talking, which made me wonder how much you had agreed to this.

And how coincidental was this chance meeting? She was looking for a boy, and there I was, conveniently, a Mandingo she was considering as a gift for you.

But I was probably already high on cocaine before you had even bothered to shit, shower, and shave, arriving here just in time for me to accept your proposition.

It didn't hurt that you were gorgeous, whiteboy.

I told your wife the best place to go was the women's bathroom. The stalls were small, but we could make it work.

You sat on the toilet lid, your wife behind you, perched on the tank and holding a fistful of your hair. This is how she pulled your ear to her lips, by your hair, to coo, *Is it good, baby?*

I kneeled on the floor in front of you, wishing your wife would just go away. Gazed up at your face, at your open mouth that never closed, looking for clues that you might be coming. You were a moaner, and I liked that. But I could never tell how close you were.

Your wife kept asking, *Is it good, baby?* and your face would contort in frustration.

Maybe, like me, you thought she sounded like a woman who only talked dirty when she practiced alone how to make the proper inflections with her voice and she hadn't quite perfected it yet.

After a while—though I could've gone all night—you said you didn't think you could come. You'd had too much to drink.

We tucked in our clothes, fixed our hair, wiped our mouths, and filed out of the stall. We needed some fresh air and went out to the patio. We crowded around a small cocktail table, passing a cigarette between the three of us, and after the last drag, when the cigarette had been snuffed out, we said our goodbyes.

————

And then there was you, lanky Slavic whiteboy.

We sat at the bar in Oilcan Harry's. Too close to the stage. The DJ's first set started with Jennifer Lopez's "Let's Get Loud." The once-empty dance floor welcomed beneath the strobe lights an epileptic throng of glittering, oiled-up, and otherwise wet whiteboys who hadn't yet rid themselves of a song now seven years old. You kept looking left, where I sat two stools over, between staring down at your drink or tenting your hands or drumming the bar top with your fingertips as if you were nervous, bored, or both.

I drank vodka cranberries and tallied how often you turned your attention to me.

I asked the bartender what you were drinking. Vodka with sweet-and-sour mix. I ordered a kamikaze—which was about the same, with one added ingredient, triple sec—and asked the bartender to send you one.

This usually wasn't my style, spending money on strangers, but you seemed like you'd been cast out by someone you loved and were looking for a place to lay your head. Like in the movies.

You accepted the drink and moved to the empty stool beside me.

You said thanks, and we took our shots.

For an hour, we made small talk, though we had to yell over the bass and the whooping from the dance floor. We repeated ourselves often, drawing our faces closer and closer until our lips grazed the rims of our ears, the conversation soon becoming more than about trying to hear what the other said.

We drank more shots: purple hooter shooters, lemon drops, chocolate cakes, pineapple upside-down cakes, hairy nipples, sex on the beaches. We kept yelling over the bass.

You said your name was Anna.

I said, That's a girl's name.

It's the name of a king, you said.

I'm a king's name, I said. A Persian king.

You're Persian? you said.

No. I'm black, I said.

You said you emigrated from Slovakia.

I said I was from Tennessee.

You said you wanted to dance with me.

I said we should have more shots, wait until the floor was less crowded.

I lied and said you looked like a whiteboy named Ari who had gone to middle school with me. You favor him, I said. At the time, I didn't think I liked whiteboys. I liked Ari, though.

What's wrong with whiteboys? you said.

I shrugged.

In middle school, we used to say whiteboys smelled like wet popcorn, I said. But Ari smelled like Cool Water cologne.

Do I smell like wet popcorn? you said.

But before I could answer, you swallowed my mouth in yours.

You pulled away, put your lips to my ear, rested your forehead against my temple. I closed my eyes, expecting to feel your tongue, but instead, you whispered, I'm HIV positive. And then you were silent.

I took you home that night. And several nights after that.

We didn't share any of the dangerous fluids, as we say.

No blood, no semen.

You were still strung out on some other dude.

You said I couldn't fuck you.

But oral sex was okay. Spooning. Kissing. That was fine.

Penetration meant cheating, you said.

I just want to know where you went. Where you are now.

The more time you spent with me, the more desperate it seemed you wanted to be with someone else.

Then one night, you couldn't get him on the phone, so you said you needed to go. You thought something terrible had happened.

You were screaming in a hushed voice so you wouldn't wake my housemates, rouse the dog. You said, I have to find him.

I tried to get you to stay. I snatched your black jean jacket away from you.

You begged me to give it back.

It was two or three in the morning and so chilly outside. But I wouldn't give it to you.

You started to go anyway, and I couldn't let you walk out into that cold air, so I gave you back your jacket.

You walked toward South First Street. You were a man in love, heartbroken and afraid. Probably regretful. You told me once that you'd wished you had waited to fall for *the one*, that person who lit up your face when he spoke your name. We'd just finished stroking each other off.

I didn't get it, thinking you'd have to be stricken with HIV to hold so tightly to romantic ideas like that.

I didn't know if I was being cynical or behaving like the worst person for you to be with.

I wanted to say I'm sorry as I stood in the doorway and watched you disappear around the corner. I couldn't say why I was standing there, except to remember the last place I saw you before I never saw you again.

Part V

CODE BLUE
THEATER

I don't want to be
the living dead
pacified with drugs
and sex.

—Essex Hemphill
"For My Own Protection"

Delirium Tremens

t's the body's yearning to be sober. The first bead of sweat forming at the temple. It's subtle tremors in the limbs, a forewarning quake even the animals sense and hence the stampede. It's lying restless the way electrocution makes one restless. And hair of the dog won't subdue it. It's covering the mouth when the volume's turned to shrill in the third circle of hell. It's gluttony's flame engulfing the skin like parchment one's sin is writ upon. It's light splintering behind the eyes. It's fever's encroachment. It's phosphene trickery, prisoner's cinema in a blacked-out room, and not a sliver of fluorescence. It's cowering beneath sheets, praying to God. It's the absence of God. It's the lion's share of disasters. A tree fallen across live wires, magnificent sparks that burn a village to the ground. It's everything that aspires to flicker. It's imagining these catastrophes. Citizens woebegone for the sake of their homes, burnt-edge leaves scattering the ground. It's everyone fallen to their knees, raking their past into charred hands, sorting through all the old feelings that made them happy at last. It's no more to show for it. It's *this never happened*. Body's betrayal enlisting a mind not intact. It's slowly breaking down, cauterized from years of chronic drinking and pill popping, toppling one's reserve when the bottle's empty. It's shrinking to corners when hallucinogens pull shadows from the walls like demon hieroglyphs come alive. It's marionettes with severed strings, delirium tremens through the flesh all the way through to the toes curled in anguish. It's bones cracking under the weight of pain. The inability to distinguish one fiery pulse from another. It's howling all the same. It's crawling the bed. It's a wrecking crew's steel ball swinging. It's disassembling one from the inside out and no doubt about suffering. It's the ravishing one must endure. It's healing.

Rogue Soldier

took the dog out for a walk one early Tuesday morning before work. Neighbors had already begun slowly emerging from their houses to stand on their porches, some in bathrobes with coffee in hand, some a newspaper, some to gather a sense of the weather or simply gaze at the pale light hovering over the mountains in the distance, which made the morning appear colorless, the way a palette might still retain stains of a previous effort to paint a canvas.

We were all smiles and good mornings and doin' just fines.

No one, least of all me, imagined that trouble burrowed beneath the brambles and brush that kept parts of Rosedale Avenue unkempt.

But trouble was there and probably had been for some time, looming in a relatively small area of land at the top of a steep hill that descended all the way to the backyards of the neighbors who lived below us.

It was there in what we thought was just torn-up grass and sticks bundled together like shredded basket weavings.

It was there, as unassuming as apples concealing razor blades in their cores.

And it found me there after the dog left clumps of shit on the ground and kicked up the already broken grass to mark the territory as ours.

But it was not ours.

I tugged the leash to pull the dog away from a scent that had his nose mired in the earth. He was too strong and stubborn, so I relented and let him linger, listening to him snort as he attempted to root out the source of the smell.

I turned my eyes to the sky to decide whether the pale light—an almost haze—indicated rainfall later on. But I couldn't tell.

Come on, Fry, I said.

I was loud and had grown annoyed, but I was instantly apologetic when he looked at me, hiding the whites of his eyes, which told me he too was sorry for whatever he had done.

Perhaps having heard the raised pitch in my voice, a small flock of blackbirds took sudden flight from the telephone wires above us. They offered a proposition, nevertheless. Four of them, I counted, were heading south toward Morningside

Park. I considered, by way of apology, walking Fry there to keep him out a bit longer before being shut in most of the day while I was at work. But we could only go as far as the Alex Haley statue and then back home again. I tugged the leash gentler this time, and Fry knew it was time to go. He scraped up one last clod of dirt and grass, digging in deep with his hind legs so the air filled with an explosion of debris, and trotted away to join me at my side.

And that's when I saw them in a flurry, summoned from beneath the ground—one, two, five, seven became a swarm of yellowjackets, designated sentinels sent to attack. They targeted my mouth first with their bites and their stings, as if to muffle the cries lodged in my throat. My lips became more and more tender as their assault grew more incessant, as if they were a mallet upon a slab of beef.

A rogue soldier aimed for my left eye; it landed on my cheek before it crawled inside the bottom eyelid to the subcutaneous tissue.

I crushed it and felt the explosion of its body, the stinging, unmerciful pain.

I had to escape, but it seemed there was none.

They had been provoked, and they were not bees. They could sting and bite, and they would never die.

So I ran away with arms flailing, the leash held high so Fry could keep pace. We ran past the rottweiler, the poodle, the pit bulls all roving inside their chain-linked fences excited by the commotion, barking and jumping against their enclosures as if to barrel them down to join Fry and me.

I pulled up my shirt to shield my face and head, and looking down, I saw Fry fearless, an exuberant puppy nearing seven years old alongside me with his ears flopping, pink tongue dangling from his mouth, practically smiling.

Why weren't they attacking him?

If there were any neighbors still on their porches, they offered no help, not even a little. I was on my own.

But I made it home, finally. The attack was over.

And I was allergic to those motherfuckers.

———

How do you medicate swelling pain except with antihistamines; vodka on ice; many vodkas on ice; a cold compress; more vodka on ice until the mind becomes apathetic, the body anesthetized, unmoving so it may rest? I spent hours learning to see through one eye; I drank more vodka on ice until I could slip into a deep sleep.

From midnight to 4:00 a.m.: restlessness, periodic vodkas on ice; my left eye swollen shut and rendered useless; but still, more vodka on ice, more antihistamines; sleep might be a dangerous commodity; seeing might be a handicap when I tried to walk a straight line; surroundings were dizzying; the world tilted off its axis when I tried to dial a number.

———————

When she answered the phone, her *hello* was all breathy consonants, no vowel sounds. It was after five in the morning.

Mama ... , I said.

Twenty minutes later, she pulled up to my house, flashing the hazards. She shook her head at me. Can you even see?

A little, I said.

When we arrived at the emergency room, a skeleton crew made up the staff who wafted casually in and out of the automatic doors from hallways just around the corners. Their presence was the only proof that yes, they were open for business.

I expected at any moment to see the entrance doors thrust open by two men, one crutched on the shoulder of the other with so much blood gushing from him, and *then* everyone would shift into gear like an ER was supposed to operate. A wheelchair would be whisked forward while a doctor tripped over himself hollering, *Sir! Sir! Sir!* his lab coattails flailing behind him, his stethoscope a noose around his neck about to slip off. The corridor would fill with squeaking rubber soles on the floor, reminding me of the basketball courts at the downtown YMCA where I'd often loitered at the gymnasium windows to watch the guys, sweaty and panting, in a game of shirts and skins.

But all was quiet, and I was quite delirious after the cocktail of yellowjacket stings, Benadryl, and vodka. I could barely walk to the check-in counter without help.

I stood braced against the counter with my pulverized face presented to a lady in paisley scrubs who pointed to where (*here, here, here . . .*) on the forms I needed to fill in my information. She handed me a pen, and something in my brain broke, like a synapse had unloosed a finned neuron that swam in circles.

I didn't know how to hold the damned thing.

It seemed right to grip it in my fist, but then that felt wrong. This was how you held a pen if you wanted to stab someone.

I couldn't get it right, so I turned the pen horizontally, but that looked wrong too. Back the other way, I slid my hand down to the ballpoint and did the best I could to write my name, phone number, address, emergency contact, insurance.

I handed back the forms, and she looked them over, looked back at me as if to determine if my scribbling was evidence I'd probably just had a stroke right in front of her and she didn't know it until now. She told me to take a seat.

I walked to a row of chairs near the entrance where Mama waited for me, half-raised from her seat.

I asked her where she was going.

She needed to get her sweater from the car.

You stay cold, I said.

She left, and I sat rocking in my seat, something inside me revving. I searched the room for Mama (*You know I just left*, I could hear her saying), and everything floated in slow motion.

I lifted my arm as if it might reach back to the car and tug her by the shoulder to get her attention and bring her back, but it was too late. I knew it when I sensed myself tilting toward an incredibly bright floor, as if an entire room had been mopped with light. I turned my face away to avoid it, twisting my head toward the entrance doors, looking for Mama, needing her to catch me because I was—

———

Dictated by: Dr. Anand N. Patel, MD
10/25/2015

04:57   Patient initially presented complaining of having been stung by a bee about 1400 yesterday. He awoke with marked facial swelling and lip swelling. He denies respiratory symptoms in triage. Shortly after he was put through, he was found on the floor actively seizing

*with generalized tonic-clonic activity. He appeared
to have sustained a tongue laceration and became
very tachycardic during this, but this settled down as
he settled down. Onset: the symptoms/episode began/
occurred acutely, yesterday, at 1400. At this time have
limited information from the patient. His mother states
he has no history of seizure activity. She did not think
he uses any illicit substances. The only medication she is
aware of him taking last night was Benadryl . . .*

———

I was on a gurney with bodies rushing around me, shouting in
clipped medic-speak. My side hurt. I was bleeding. I wanted
to know what had happened. Nobody told me anything.
They saw what had happened but wouldn't share it with me.
No sympathy.

I tried to stay alert, but I grew too groggy to muster.

Muscle couldn't keep.

Much longer.

———

*Dictated By: Dr. Abigail Deguzman, MD
10/25/2015
06:08   Patient found at 0552 on the floor, bleeding from the
           mouth in room 15. He had been placed in room and*

tech went to get Dinamap to obtain vitals, and during that time patient fell onto the floor. Patient was then witnessed to have seizure with Dr. Barbee present, the second one since patient was presented. Patient was placed onto backboard and transferred to gurney. Patient was administered medications after starting IV to the left forearm. During the encounter, the patient had a prolonged period of postictal combativeness. He was very uncooperative and so was given multiple doses of Ativan to settle down. Efforts are somewhat hampered by him pulling out several of his IVs over the course of our attempts to medicate him. Patient was restrained by several staff until 0610 when he calmed down enough to not thrash in the bed . . .

———

Flat on my back, one eye rolled inside my head while too much light tried to wreck my one good cornea. I turned away from the light, felt the weight of gravity, dense and heavy, like swimming in amniotic fluid. I smiled and reached up my hand toward a body.

You ready to go in the spaceship? she said.

I'm ready, I said.

Slowly, I began moving—*stay very still, okay?*—into a tube while someone played Simon, filling the room entirely with the noise of pressed buttons, the inability to follow suit, repeating the patterns wrong wrong wrong—*stay still, sweetie.* I held my breath, agitated, because it seemed the thing to do encased inside that tube, to prevent the white coats from instructing me, *don't move, be still, you're doing just fine.*

I was inside the MRI machine *now . . . really can't move now . . . spiked my body with something more potent now since I know I'm here in the machine now, hard plastic digging into my shoulders, shit hurts now, sucked in tube now, screwed in waiting, ready to go now, but now, now, now I is drowsy more now like now now am I drunk life? What's that stuff*—hold tight—*now, who says, now . . . here now in MRI . . .*

———

Lifting forward, a hand pressed me gently back down; a sudden light brightened as I was brought out from inside the machine.

The room was cold, and I had only a thin hospital gown to cover me.

I shoved my hands, up to the forearms, between my thighs to keep warm.

We're taking you to your room now.

Thank you, I said.

I was wheeled away on a gurney toward the elevator.

The bell dinged, but when the elevator opened, it sounded like the fake elevator doors on those 1970s TV shows that always got stuck in the tracks and wouldn't close right.

Up we went, though the cables seemed cautious, as if someone, hand over fist, was pulling us slowly to our floor.

I wanted to tell the orderly how I'd predicted I'd be here. But he didn't know me, even if I needed him to so I could say out loud: I'm in this hospital because I have a serious problem or else I'd be dead. I knew this yesterday; I knew this a week ago. Months ago I knew this.

He wheeled me into my room, where a TV glowed dimly, the volume turned low. Someone else is already here—a nurse—I thought, and together, wasting no time— on three, she said—they transferred me to the bed, and the orderly left. The nurse's shape flitted across my slit-eyes to hook me to monitors and an IV.

You're not gonna pull these out again, are you? she said.

I moved my head side to side.

Good. Doctor will be in to see you soon.

———

Dictated by: Dr. Abigail Deguzman, MD
10/25/2015
07:27   Originally, I saw the patient today at about 0608. He
*   had delirium tremens and a bee sting for which Statcare*

was asked to admit. However, there was concern for orbital fracture and inferior rectus muscle. At that time, I was told there is no Ophthalmology here at Physicians Regional Medical Center. I just now spoke to Dr. Dawson, who is courtesy staff here. His office is beside North Knoxville Medical Center with East Tennessee Eye Surgeons. Due to the nature of the case, he was able to come see the patient, thankfully. The patient has restriction with extraocular muscles. The eye dilated fine. The pupil does not react, but this could be temporary damage to iris constrictor muscles due to the fracture sustained during seizure. I spoke with Dr. Dawson and now with Dr. Collins in the emergency room where the seizure occurred, and given that this has been resolved, we can move forward with appropriately admitting the patient to Statcare Internal Medicine to deal with those other issues.

———

You buggered up good, huh, bud? Mama said, her wet thumb scrubbing the corner of my mouth. More dried blood.

Two seizures, she said.

I didn't speak.

Said your alcohol level was *excessive.*

Mama was a nurse too, and when she told me this, it sounded clinical and maternal at the same time. It was hard for me to know which of her roles was speaking. She put so much emphasis on *ex-ces-SIVE*, an inflection that could sometimes be a warning I was about to get smacked upside the head, or sometimes a caution, the way a doctor might say to a patient's mother: either he quits, or he dies.

Excessive. A whisper when I said it, so I turned my face to meet her eyes, to tell her that I knew.

She smoothed my blankets as she returned to her chair by the TV to make a call. The only person I knew who still had a flip phone in 2015 was my mother. It glowed in her face with such brightness she must have constantly extended and retracted her arm to dial a number, to tilt her chin up to peer down her nose at the screen and squint with her finger poised to press the right digits.

Yeah, I'm still here at the hospital, she said to someone on the other end. He's in a room now.

She tried to mouth to me who it was. I flipped my palms in the air and huffed since I couldn't read her lips. She dismissed me with a hand wave, her mouth pursed as if to say, *Boy, go on somewhere.*

So I did. I went with the IV drip. Though it didn't carry me too far from her. She was still there . . . there in the chair, leaning back as I'd seen her do so often at home: legs crossed at the ankles, left arm tucked high under the right, her hand cradling the phone against her head that was tilted just enough to loosen the muscles in her neck.

She was there in the lights flickering inside the machinery attached to me, in the TV and cell phone's glow emanating from her head; she was there when my lids flitted open to make sure she was always there as the drip eased me into much-needed, restful sleep, sinking from the full weight of exhaustion until I felt in its totality my ravaged body beginning, truly, to convalesce there in that dim corner of a hospital room, Mama there across from my bed, babbling in a hushed, lilting voice that—*bless his heart*—I was falling asleep and that she felt less worried now, so she could sit there in *who knows what time it is* and stifle a laugh to keep from waking me, catch her breath, and just sit there with her friend on the phone, insisting over and over, *Girl, stop*, until, there, now, she did.

Discipline

One day, when I was just a kid, Daddy and I worked outside in the backyard, quietly taking clothes off the line and folding them into a basket.

When we finished, we headed back inside.

Daddy paused, looked to the sky, noticing a migrating flock of geese.

He admired how their two lines angled to a fine point, forming a perfect letter, and said that birds in flight were more in line than any of the rest of us.

But then, one of the geese near the back veered too far from the rest, and the whole formation began to crumble.

Daddy's jaw grew tense. Get back in line, he grumbled, as if it were the bad seed in the family.

And the bird tightened, reforming the design, and framed a patch of sky so flawlessly it might have fallen, a gift, at Daddy's feet.

We watched until that letter of geese vanished into the distance.

Daddy waited, perhaps to ensure the formation remained intact.

I waited to enter the house behind him.

They were just geese to me. I was too young then to appreciate how they could go anywhere the sky would lead them and not even the brow of the sun could melt their wings.

Homecoming

fter five days detoxing in the hospital, it was so wonderful to be back home in the old neighborhood again. How the sunlight hung in the trees. Like toilet paper strewn in good-natured tomfoolery. How the streets were paved with speed bumps now, tall as hurdles, castaway trash in the sewers, thigh-high grass yellowing in the yards, especially the house on the corner, its basement so flooded you could see inside the gaping hole on the side, the mortar crumbling like sand sifting through someone's fingers . . . oh, what a glorious day to come home!

And I was five days sober!

The old neighbors had neither moved away nor died—it was too good to be true—and those crafty sons-of-bitches were beaming ear to ear, so happy to see me. I'd have to remember to keep the curtains parted lest they have trouble peeping in my bedroom window to glimpse what new beau I'd be bringing home—just like in the old days.

And the new neighbors were a rousing bunch, indeed, particularly the woman two houses down, who, earlier that morning, I had almost introduced myself to except she was busy breaking up with her boyfriend. He had dreadlocks that roped to his shoulders, which probably tickled your nose when you leaned in close to him, smelling perhaps of sandalwood, and his dark skin glowed as if he generously applied cocoa butter all over his body every single day. And why again was she breaking up with him?

Surely not because he wore a wifebeater long enough to stretch over his ass, his pants ill-fitted to contain everything. How resourceful and what a sense of fashion, that man, leaning against a black Mazda where a door was rusted through and the tailpipe and the fender and the roof almost entirely rusted through. The rims on that car, of course, were all silvery opalescent and gave underappreciated meaning to *prioritization*.

But *her* . . . oh, she was too good to be true: a voice like a drag queen's cursing, I could almost imagine her tripping over a power cord and the *goddamn, you* she was sure to spit out, bemoaning the day its creator was ever born.

She had what we called *womanosity*. When he told her, You kicked *me* out, remember? She responded, You got that right, muthafucka!

SNAP!

Oh, why did I ever leave?

I forgot we're family-centric here.

A little girl who I presume was her daughter, barely tall enough to reach the porch rail, stood just as I did, looking back and forth between them, learning multiple contexts for four-letter words. She sucked her thumb, tugging her earlobe as if to open the ear canal a little wider to receive this new vocabulary. I could imagine her one day on a Saturday morning watching *SpongeBob SquarePants* in the living room, laid out on the floor with a bowl of cereal in one hand and a spoon in the other, becoming fluent in how to say with perfect conviction: Bitch! I want a crabby patty!

By now, the couple had attracted a crowd, the streets lined with every resident. Even the neighbors two blocks away ran over, envious of how skillfully we could attract the police so early in the morning.

That's when I lost interest and returned inside. This was not the type of behavior I should be so engrossed in.

I only last night had started AA again, and what a gorgeous night it was, with the supermoon a wonderful distraction from the otherwise pale faces (made paler in the moonlight) of the recovering.

We all watched it through the windows of a church's multipurpose room, sipping coffee, Diet Coke—anything caffeinated really—to keep the superhighways inside our bodies busy with traffic.

Sitting in folding chairs, we engaged in the usual protocols, introduced ourselves, belabored points of honesty.

We were addicts, all of us, grieving our ill wills, our lost battles, our messy beds damp from night sweats. Someone was always speaking, but all eyes were awash in the glow of the moon.

A woman grabbed my arm as if inhabiting a sudden flashback to headlights of an oncoming car and no time to steer out of its way.

A man nodded into his empty Styrofoam cup, tearing the rim to a jagged, half-moon edge; saying *yes* so quietly, his lip quivering, it seemed almost too apparent it was too soon to discuss what all had happened in his life.

No one remarked how lucky we were, though, for the moon tonight, how its soft light was a gentle kiss upon the eyelids. No one gave themselves over to this higher power, nor to be pulled into its slow dance so that you scarcely knew you were moving, like falling unwittingly in love with a man with dreadlocks who smelled of sandalwood, whose hair roped to his shoulders and tickled your nose when you leaned in close to him, so close.

Oh, to be happy for once without the constant threat of memory.

I wanted to share with them how I once fucked a man while a police car's spotlight shone through the rear window of the car we were in, in the parking lot of a prestigious southern university; how it was thrilling to be straddling him in the front seat while the light of the afterlife engulfed us.

Yes, some might have died of embarrassment or the fear of jail. But not us.

I wanted to share how we kept going, despite the officer approaching with his flashlight sweeping across the fogged window. How he peered in so dangerously close it might as well have been a threesome when we rolled the window down, revealing our sweat, our breathless heaving chests, our funky interloping bodies.

How he stared at us and placed a hand on his nightstick—and this was no euphemism.

He gave us a pass—told us simply to move on, that we were trespassing.

I wanted the room to laugh at how young, how obscene we were, to insinuate either the officer was kind or perhaps aroused, that perhaps he even drove home with one hand on the wheel, the other on the cruiser's rigid gear shift, thinking of all the things he could do to himself.

I wanted blue moon faces screaming *yes yes yes*, to be the straw that broke the miserable camel's back, the straw incinerated like a meth lab poorly attended to.

I wanted them to wink, to nod as strangers do when they mean to say, *Thanks, I needed that*, the way anonymous sex used to be such a gift.

That night, the lunar light was a marvel we should have all been equally beholden to, perhaps encouraged to fall in love again gazing out the window, bent almost to falling from our chairs, internally combusting from such gratuitous beauty, and this man with his Styrofoam cup would no longer be ruined by his silence and say, *To hell with it*, and then go around the circle kissing every woman he'd ever fantasized spending an evening with, tangled in a blanket on the football field of his old high school, imagining himself a teenager scoring his first lay like the rest of the popular kids beneath the black silk sheet of night while the brightest, unblinking eye watched.

Code Blue Theater

You were the one whiteboy who came over to visit a house where usually there were only blackfolk. You were friends with Andre—my boyfriend—his former coworker at the nursing home where he worked as a dietary cook. You extended your hand, not to give me dap, or to pull me into a bro hug, or even to change the shape of your hand for a fist bump, but to clasp my palm, as in a transaction.

You didn't say *wassup* or *what it do*, but *nice to meet you.*

Your name was Dylan, and you were tall with dirty blond hair, blue eyes, a chipped tooth. And some might say you were cute.

You drank Natural Light, smoked cigarettes and weed if it was passed your way.

You were addicted to opioids, but you'd been trying to quit, especially after your girlfriend quit you; she was a CNA where you and Andre worked, but when you wouldn't let the pills go after dating for a while, she let you go. You left the nursing home not long after that.

One day, three years later, when I was home in Knoxville on spring break from graduate school at the University of Iowa, I watched you overdose.

It happened on a Friday afternoon, when you were supposed to be cutting the grass in the backyard, even though the sky was gray and steadily darkening with threats of a rainstorm.

I had planned to spend the day with Andre binge-watching Netflix, but company kept coming.

Bree was the first, announcing herself by popping her Dubble Bubble gum.

You came in right after her, pulling a lawn mower behind you like a wagon, holding on to the handle with one hand while jostling a can of Natural Light in the other. By the time you made it to the dining room—where Bree and I were sitting—you'd left a trail of beer that foamed on the hardwood floor.

You better clean that shit up before Andre sees it, Bree said.

You looked back at the spillage and mouthed *fuck*.

Get the mop, dude, she said when you stood there gaping at the mess you'd made. The way she exaggerated the *u* in *dude* made it seem as if what she'd really said was, *Get the mop, you dumb, triflin' ass, muthafucka.* Bree was harsh, and if you didn't know it already, you got on her nerves.

Why didn't he just take the lawn mower around the *side* of the house? she said to me after you'd gone into the kitchen.

But you didn't go for a mop. You went for paper towels, which we could hear you tearing off in sheets.

The mop, dude, get the mop, she yelled. You wasting paper towels.

You were shrug-shouldered with humiliation when you returned with a mop to clean up the mess.

Did you wet it? You gotta wet it, Bree said, and she watched you slink off to the kitchen again.

At least you had the floor cleaned by the time Andre came back inside.

You and I would often joke about Andre's idea of what constituted clean and orderly—how he liked his place mats arranged on the dining room table with the corners touching so the center of the table was a framed rectangle; how his condiment bottles on the countertop had to be in rows by height with the labels facing out; how the chairs had to be tucked beneath the table when not in use so they weren't in the way when people moved around the room.

Andre didn't comment on the wet streaks slowly fading away on the floor. He'd decided to put some meat on the grill and went into the spare bedroom, where he kept a bag of charcoal in the closet. He dragged it through the kitchen to take outdoors. I asked him if it might rain, which was my way of saying, don't cook out because it might rain. Andre answered by asking me to season the burgers and boneless chicken breasts. I did not season the burgers and boneless chicken breasts.

Smitty was the last to show up, talking on his cell phone. I told Andre to ask him to season the burgers and boneless chicken breasts. When Smitty heard his name, he waved me off, then secluded himself in the living room, where blackout curtains created a dark alcove for him to hide in but not to muffle the conversation he was having with his soon-to-be ex-wife, whom he'd recently begun to refer to as his *baby mama*.

I heard Smitty pop the tab on a Miller Genuine Draft tall boy (the only beer he and Andre drank) and loudly slurp the spillover. Andre had told me several times during our nightly, long-distance phone calls how Smitty regretted that his marriage was breaking up and that he didn't care anymore that his wife had gotten pregnant with another man's child. Of course, the fact that he too might father a child with another woman may have given him this perspective; he might have rationalized their mutual infidelities as a mutual canceling out of wrongs: they'd both fucked up, so couldn't they just get past the drama to be parents to the one child they'd created together? He'd be by to pick her up later, I heard him say, and then his voice lowered in pitch, as if he'd cupped a hand around the mouthpiece. Come on, he said, crooning to her like an eighties balladeer in what he could never deny wasn't an attempt to, as he said, Please, baby, let me hit that.

You'd taken the lawn mower to the backyard and returned to the dining room with another twelve-ounce can of Natural Light. You popped the tab and set the can on the table beside Bree. Without taking a sip, you lingered briefly in the middle of the room and mumbled to yourself—or to Bree or me, neither of us could tell—then took off again. You returned with a leaf blower, a gas can, which you carried beneath one arm, and another Natural Light. You opened it and placed it on the mantel, then took the leaf blower and gas can to the backyard. Never once did you sip from either beer.

Bree looked up from a game she'd been playing on her cell phone to watch you leave the room and come back. Her hair, slicked down with grease, was pulled tight into a ponytail that lashed the air each time she whipped her head to follow you back and forth, a snarl stiffening her upper lip like a pinched fold of dough. Her expressiveness portrayed a three-dimensional annoyance that reminded me of the look on people's faces after they'd made a petty comment about some petty thing.

When she heard Andre in the kitchen, she went to him to ask what was wrong with you.

Andre, entering the dining room seasoning a plate of boneless chicken breasts, told her you were *on one*. He set the plate on the table to light a Black and Mild, then continued to lightly dust the meat with seasonings.

Bree asked what you were on.

Through an exhale of smoke, Andre told her he didn't know. Probably Roxys, he said, two fifteens. He clenched the tip of the plastic filter between his teeth, his right eye cinched tight to avoid the smoke, and let the tip rest in the corner of his mouth.

Two fifteens my ass, Bree said.

As if on cue, you walked in, tilting a can of Natural Light. You'd forgotten the other open, untouched cans still in their places on the table, the mantel. You tried to take a sip but missed your mouth when you stumbled, lifting your foot too high, as if you were prepared to step up and had come down thinking a landing was closer than it was, so gravity pulled you forward, which threw you off balance. You pretended to play it off with a bit of footwork you said you'd learned from watching Childish Gambino.

You need to sit down, dude, Andre said, laughing.

You fucked up, ain't you? Bree said simultaneously.

I'm awright, you said, and as if to prove this, you shook your arms and legs vigorously in the air. You seemed agitated. Your eyes were wet and tired, the rim of your lower lids puffy, pink like an albino rabbit's eyes. Your eyes wanted sleep, but your body was fueled, apparently, by thirty milligrams of pills to keep you sleepless. When you disappeared outside again, Bree told Andre she heard that you crushed your pills. Andre said yes, you did, and that you snorted the powder. Bree shook her head, her mouth pursed. She didn't snort her pills, nor anything else for that matter. Unlike you, she took pills because she had lupus. Yes, sometimes, she'd said many times before, when her lupus flared up and she could barely get out of bed, she had to call around to see if she could buy extra pills; she needed always to be in constant supply to keep the symptoms of her lupus in check.

I gotta get this meat on the grill, Andre said and grabbed the plate of boneless chicken breasts and headed outside. Smitty came in just then, and the two of them stopped just short of colliding. My bad, Smitty said. He had been in the backyard and came to tell us that you had just fuckin' threw up in the trash can.

Puttin' shit up your nose, that's what happens, Bree said. Smitty said you were outside, sweaty and red in the face. Would you put shit up your nose? Bree asked me.

Nah, I said, to imply hell no! as if I'd never dared to do something like that, ever, not ever had I smoked crack cocaine, nor did I once, when so fucked up, attempt to snort coke through the lit end of a cigarette. Obviously, Bree had forgotten I'd told her about my past drug use, about those very incidents. I searched her face for the recognition that told me she remembered, but her own eyes were glazed over with what could be either the weariness of being fed up with other people's shit or the settling in of her own high. She tapped a cigarette out of her pack and proceeded to strike a series of sparks with her lighter.

Your lighter's out of fluid, Bree, I told her, but she kept trying.

Who knows why people do what they do, she said, her head beginning to loll.

When I finally went outside, the coals were lit, and the grill was smoking. Andre paced nervously as the skirt of his black bib apron fluttered in the slight breeze, clapping a pair of tongs together like pincers in one hand and taking frequent swigs from his beer with the other. Smitty leaned against one of the posts on the small porch, giving me the side-eye when he saw me, shaking his head. It's not looking too good, he said, nodding toward something past me. I followed his gaze to where you sat in a patio chair a few feet away from the grill. I hadn't noticed you, but probably because I wasn't expecting to see you sitting with your legs shoulder-width apart, each of your arms resting along the arms of the chair, your head hanging so your chin barely touched your chest, your mouth languishing partly open with drool stretching a silvery strand down into your lap.

Andre and Smitty alternated turns calling your name. Andre tilted up your head, only for it to fall forward with a slight bob; he said you needed milk. Smitty directed our attention to the dog, Andre's pit bull, who circled you in your chair, then stopped to lie down. She whined, half-barked, then she was up again, letting loose a high-pitched squeal; she pawed at the dirt and grass, digging with her nails, sending a fretwork of dust into the air that formed a cloud around you.

Andre came back without any milk but with Bree smoking her cigarette. Oh gawd, she said, her eyes now wide open when she saw you. She said she had to leave because you were fucked up. You were a whiteboy, she said, and if one of us had to call 911, she didn't want any part in what happened when they got here.

I didn't pay Bree any attention. I watched you, wondering how many sad clowns were packed inside that tiny car.

Andre, too, paid Bree no mind because he thought you were just passing out, which was good, he said, because you needed to sleep it off.

I wasn't so sure. I went inside.

I heard Bree's thick-heeled boots not soon after, clomping into the dining room, where I'd distracted myself on the computer.

She stuttered directions for me to look up signs of an overdose on the internet. I did and listed a few symptoms to her: dilated pupils, severe difficulty or shallow breathing, gurgling sounds, blue lips or fingers, nausea or vomiting, unresponsiveness . . . a person didn't need to exhibit all the symptoms to indicate an overdose. Bree rushed outside, yelling to Andre and Smitty: vomiting, something about the pupils, gurgling in the throat, breathing with blue lips . . .

It had been roughly thirty minutes since you had unloaded your car with all the tools you needed to cut Andre's backyard, since you had danced your way out of a stumble and Andre and I had laughed, since you had popped open three cans of beer, two of which you abandoned untouched. And then you suddenly began vomiting in the garbage can and were placed in that chair. But if you had done so—we still weren't sure—how long had it been since you snorted those pills?

Bree rushed back through the house, gathering her purse and cell phone off the table, and waved goodbye.

See ya, she said. Lord willing and the creek don't rise. I'm going to get my nails done.

I set the laptop aside, feeling uneasy. I needed to see for myself how bad it had gotten for Bree to leave the way she had.

I felt as if I were about to open a door into a past that often haunted me, entering a room to lift a sheet covering a body that lay cold on a slab. *Was it me?*

I became a visitor in a place I hadn't been to in a while. Even though I recognized the familiar surroundings, I felt like a stranger, and it was possible that you, too, felt like a stranger inside your own body.

I'm coming, I'm coming, was the reluctant way I walked through the rooms to get outdoors.

I approached the backyard and heard music that hadn't been playing before. I smelled mesquite smoke mixed with charred chicken flesh and seasoning that didn't waft on the subtle breeze before, and I saw the opaque clouds billowing from the grill that before had been a cloud of dust the dog had kicked up. But this new cloud blocked you from my view.

This was the moment I pretended that I didn't wait too long to follow my intuition; that I didn't need to suspect a bad situation even when your slack-jawed mouth drooled with so many silvery, silken strands of spit; that you weren't propped up like a mannequin to model normality; that you weren't trying to convince us you were only having a bad trip (but nothing you couldn't shake off); that this was you just playing possum.

Andre used his cell phone to record you while he and Smitty kept calling your name. But you couldn't answer them.

Your arms had gone limp, no longer resting on the chair. Your hands were likewise motionless between your thighs. You breathed, but your breathing was labored, shallow gasping, as if the air was trapped so deep inside your chest that when it reached my ears, it was the echo of your efforts to breathe that I heard, your lungs taking in breath but sending back the faint noise of rattling cans.

You were in tremors, as if from shocks of low-voltage electricity, as if your body was a city of dimming lights from a series of rolling brownouts.

You were shutting down.

Your face was blue with the encroachment of more blue—your lips blue, your cheeks besieged with blue, an armada of blue storming toward the north theater of your face, capillaries carrying the blue until the totality of your face would be subsumed by it, and Smitty and Andre acted as if they didn't know whether to continue to barbeque, to wait and see what happened, or to do as I said and fucking call 911.

I couldn't stop looking at you. I wouldn't blink. If I didn't blink, you'd be fine. You'd be fine because *I* was fine, because I was proof that rock bottom didn't need to mean death.

I'd come down off the pipe once and struggled through the night, shivering. No amount of blanketing would qualm it, and nothing could distract me from believing that as I lay in a bed demonized by crack cocaine, I felt elsewhere the heels of so many people walking back and forth across the future site of my grave.

I had to believe that Smitty didn't want to call 911 because he was a felon who didn't want cops swarming with their detective work.

Andre was afraid that he might be wrong about you having a bad trip and that you were dying while he drank beer, recording you while he made sure the boneless chicken breasts were neither overcooked nor raw in the middle. He was afraid, the way we all were, that this wasn't the movies, where the blue in your face was special-effects makeup and magic.

We heard sirens coming from St. Mary's Hospital a few blocks away. Within minutes, three paramedics climbed out of a fire truck and, together, walked casually to the backyard.

Back here? one said, pointing.

Yes, back here, I said, swinging my arm like a propeller to rush them.

The first paramedic knelt beside you, took his fist, and rubbed circles over your heart. The second asked us your name. When we told him, he asked you if you could hear him. What'd you take today? he asked. Your response carried the same low gurgling you'd been making since Andre dialed 911. Shaking his head, the paramedic repeated the question.

The third paramedic started an IV and gave your vitals to the second EMT, who wrote them down on his gloved hand. The glove was blue, and I worried the ink wouldn't show. I came closer when the first paramedic shone his tiny flashlight into your eyes to check your pupils. They were small as pinpoints. The whites of your eyes waxy.

Two cops arrived and immediately began gathering details. The first cop took information from one of the paramedics while the second spoke with Andre. Andre told the cop that you admitted taking two fifteens of Roxys, but he believed you had taken more than that or that you had taken something else with it. The first paramedic stopped rubbing your chest to interrupt their conversation. He agreed with Andre, so the cop asked if you were ever in the house. First, Andre said no, then he backtracked and said instead that you had been unloading the lawn mower from your truck and had started to bring it through the house before he stopped you and asked that you bring the lawn mower around the house to the backyard. I worried he was implicating himself too much because he was so desperate for you not to be in the house in his version of events. He didn't want to give the cops probable cause to search inside.

Smitty had been quiet, shrinking back, his eyes suspiciously watching the cops. He saw me looking for him, and when our eyes locked, he mouthed, *That's the cop.* It took him a few times mouthing and gesturing at the cop for me to understand what he meant. Smitty had been in a minor car accident just around the corner from Andre's house a few weeks earlier. But he didn't have a driver's license. The cop wrote him a ticket, and that seemed to be the end of it. But seeing him now, at the house, was too much of a coincidence. It incited a nervous fear within Smitty that showed on his face.

I walked over to tell Smitty I didn't think the cop recognized him. He was too busy explaining to Andre how people would sometimes ask to use the bathroom so they could take drugs. That's why he wanted to know if you were in the house. He needed a timeline of events. But everyone's conversations were put on hold when, suddenly, you leaned forward so abruptly in your chair you nearly fell out of it. Two of the paramedics had to catch you and press you back into the chair. Easy, easy, Dylan, they said.

You shook your head, looked around to familiarize yourself, and as if none of this had ever happened, responded to a barrage of questions. You verified your name, spelled your last name that had earlier given Andre trouble. You gave your address. And, finally, because you were cold, you asked for a blanket.

In a minute, a paramedic said.

Curiously, though, no one asked you what you'd taken. They loaded you onto a gurney with a blue blanket. You wrapped it around yourself, including your head. Your muffled voice asked what hospital they were taking you to.

It's wherever you want to go, a paramedic said.

You said St. Mary's since it was closest to your house.

As they wheeled you away, Andre closed the lid on the grill to suffocate the still red-hot coals. I took the chair you sat in and stacked it with the others. A smear of blood on the armrest had to be wiped away. Smitty wanted to leave but was afraid to get in his car and drive home. Across the street, where you'd parked your car, the two original police officers were joined by two more squad cars and a K-9 unit. It had grown dark by then. Flashlights lit the interior of your car while a German shepherd was taken by the leash to sniff around and eventually inside your vehicle. I'd forgotten they had your car keys. After you were taken away, Andre found them; they must have fallen from your pocket at some point, hidden in the high grass. One of the police officers asked to take them.

You came back to the house a few hours later. Andre and I were playing a game of spades with some friends—the JJs, Jay and Jalisa—who arrived shortly after the cops had put away their flashlights and left. Andre showed them the video he'd taken of you earlier in the chair. Jalisa had been rolling a blunt, and Jay was smoking a cigarette, and both of them watched with their mouths agape at the blue, drooling face gurgling ceaselessly before the camera.

As they watched the video, I replayed that sudden intake of breath that brought you back to seemingly full vitality. Narcan, I was told, was what the paramedic administered through the IV. They said it took about two minutes to revive you. Two more minutes without it, you might have been dead.

You had come back to ask Andre to let you keep your lawn equipment in his backyard, to tell him privately that you'd taken heroin earlier that day, and to thank him for calling 911. Andre must have told you I was the one who told him to.

On your way out, you said, Thank you, Darius, avoiding my eyes, though you briefly squeezed my shoulder. Andre walked you to the door and returned quickly to the table to deal the cards for another hand. We beat the JJs that night, but that was probably because they'd gotten too high smoking the blunt to pay attention.

Part VI

YOU DON'T HAVE TO LIKE IT

Do you think I could walk pleasantly
and well-suited toward annihilation?
with a scrotal sack full
of primordial loneliness
swinging between my legs
like solid bells?

—Essex Hemphill
"Heavy Breathing"

Incubus

was nearing my late twenties when I finally stopped playing the generous host to all the pretty boys who wanted to enter the pleasure dome in less than full regalia. And now, a decade later, I fear I might be stuck with the *ick*; there's a tickle in my throat that won't go away. I force myself to laugh as if this might clear the festering obstruction lodged in my airway; I can breathe, but I have a devil of a time; I feel choked up, thinking it might be possible my blood is streaming with razor wire inside my body. A part of me wants to hunker down and pray that I survive, but I seldom do—pray, that is—except on occasion and usually in a moment of duress. And what greater time would that be than now, when the prospect of living with the *ick* brings me so much stress. I hope it doesn't mean I'm cursed to death for my—how shall I put it?—past *activities*. Imagine a pair of lips slightly parted, tongues rapt with aphasia, bodies curled serpentine one moment, and the next, hands pressing faces hard against iced-over windows, open mouths warming the glass with ecstatic breath, leaving fading impressions against the panes. I do. Such is the life of an incubus, of two men—and another, and still more— who long to be heaved together in a clearing on a balmy night, bejeweled with sweat, and hour after hour they undress night's recriminations, they leave it bare, they want an incubus to no longer be a demon but an answered prayer.

No Limits

This is how I began, slowly, to annihilate myself, beginning with Perry, a man gorgeously mixed with redbone-black and Dominican blood, who was a sensitive romantic, and despite him being a Pisces—the water to my fire—I was desperate for a boyfriend and prayed he could be him. We met in an internet chatroom in 2000 or 2001, some America Online cesspool, when, at the time, I was trying to escape Nashville—his hometown—where I attended Tennessee State University while he was a student at the University of Tennessee in Knoxville, my hometown. We found this hilariously ironic when we learned this about one another during our first phone conversation, which was when I also became nagged by thoughts that he most likely wouldn't pass for straight in mixed company; his brand of masculinity reminded me of men who were actually straight but who everyone was convinced were gay. And since I hadn't come out yet, I worried I would need to keep him at arm's length in the light of day, having grown increasingly nervous the more we continued our back and forth over the internet, the intermittent phone calls taken in the privacy of my dorm room closet, outside the earshot of my roommates, carrying on this way for several weeks until we finally agreed to meet in person when I visited home for a weekend.

Perry suggested that the UT campus would be a good place to link up, so we did, taking an early evening walk around the grounds. We bided our time mostly making small talk, saying the same things over and over as we searched for somewhere secluded to truly test our compatibility, even if we wouldn't admit it out loud, circling the subject of fucking—or anything remotely close to sensual touching—as if we were tethered by a thread that neither of us seemed willing to break.

Eventually, we arrived at a creek bed bordered by bushes and persimmon trees. This is my spot, he said. But it was only semiprivate. I worried about several maintenance facilities nearby, which were busy with employees on the evening shift who might see us as they took their coffee and cigarette breaks outside the buildings; we were also too close to Cumberland Avenue, the campus's main drag, where it was possible a turning car's headlights might swing our way and expose us.

So now what? I said.

You know what? he said, taking me by the tips of my fingers. And we dropped to the grass, kissing and groping each other, the streetlights trapped in the branches, struggling to reach us in the dark cul-de-sac of bushes and tree trunks we thought we'd be safe hiding inside—which we were, if only we made the best of our time. And so, with what little light that made it through the branches to brighten Perry's face, I read whatever expression might be visible there and what it might say about how far he was willing to let me go. But when I tried to put a hand down his pants, he stopped me. I wasn't sure if it was because of the risk of being outdoors or if he wanted to take things more slowly. I placed my hands loosely on his hips; tentatively, I moved my mouth against his lips with a little tongue, my eyes open, tense with skepticism, roving the tops of the trees to find the seam where the green turned black against a barely lit sky.

————

I transferred to the University of Tennessee the next year, and Perry and I decided to share a dorm room. For both of us, we realized we looked better on paper, so it made sense for us to be just friends and, eventually, besties who occasionally kissed on the lips.

But this isn't about the grand times Perry and I had as roommates. If anything, that experience proved that not only were we not compatible as romantic companions but we also didn't make compatible roommates. We agreed we must never live together again. And we did just that, eventually moving into our own separate apartments, even if they were in the same complex.

But one day, even this proximity would prove too close. Summer was ending, triggering the beginning of the fall semester. I was taking a bag of garbage to the dumpster, and on my way back to my apartment, I heard Perry calling my name. When I turned around, I saw him walking toward me with someone else.

Come here, he said, I want you to meet somebody. And this *somebody*, who ended up standing just inches from me wearing diamond studs in his ears, a powder-blue golf shirt revealing his muscular arms, and half of a dragon sleeve tattoo contrasting boldly against his dark skin, is what this is all about.

This is one fine Negro! I thought.

He's pretty, I said, and Tycen gave me a smile so wide his nostril flared. He reminded me of Derek Luke from the movie *Antwone Fisher*.

I found it difficult to look him in the eyes, so I cast my gaze downward, told him it was nice to meet him. I glanced up briefly to give him dap, but instead, he drew me in for a hug.

He's friendly, Perry said, laughing.

Yes, indeed! I thought.

I can see, I said, then I cast my eyes down again, noticing how Tycen's tucked shirt clung to his abs, that he had nice feet inside his sandals.

He had moved from the Florida panhandle, Jacksonville, to be with Perry, which surprised me since I hadn't known Perry was pursuing anyone. He was only a month younger than Perry, so they were fellow Pisceans.

We'll have to hang out soon, I said, hurrying to get back to my apartment. Just call me, Perry.

Good to meet you, Darius, Tycen said, waving, smiling.

And as I looked back at the two of them walking away, I felt my sense of loyalty corroding. I heard Perry laughing that laugh of a man who had definitely fallen in love, whose heartbeat was probably quickening, fluttering, when Tycen's warm hand grabbed the inner flesh of his upper arm to gently pull him slightly off-kilter as they ascended the incline in the road.

I watched them, knowing as Perry must have known, that this was not desire or passion or lust. No, what Perry felt was love.

I watched them, and flashes of Tycen's sinewy muscles raced to my mind and trembled every nerve in my body with gratitude. And when I was just about ready to turn around, to quit backing away toward home because I couldn't quit watching them, but especially *him*, Tycen looked back at me, waving his hand in the air once more, his teeth gleaming through a smile, while Perry trudged forward, oblivious to this simplest of gestures, this final farewell—*hasta luego*—none the wiser that I wanted Tycen, and in all likelihood, that I would betray Perry in the worst possible way to get him.

————

The first time Tycen came over to my apartment without Perry, I hoped it was because things between them had become unbearable. Except that wasn't the case.

Perry had left for the weekend to visit his parents in Nashville, and it was too soon for Tycen to meet the parents, he said. And so he stayed behind, sitting alone in their apartment, bored.

I told him how glad I was that he was there, that we were together, alone, at last. Only I disguised my voice so it seemed theatrical, not meant to be taken seriously.

When he complimented me on my apartment (*This is gorgeous, Darius!*)—the cherry wood coffee table and bookshelves, the tufted charcoal-gray sofa and loveseat, the carpet, nothing too fancy, just orderly—I was determined to figure out a way to make it appear as if I wasn't going after him but leading him to the conclusion that he wanted me.

Come on, I said, let me take you out.

———

I introduced him to the Carousel, a gay bar near campus. When we arrived, we went up a couple of floors to where the drag show was set to begin. There were several drag queens wrapping up conversations with their friends, hurrying to get backstage. They rushed past us, some decorated in gold ropes, hoops of silver, hair up and splayed, faces blushed with pastels, luminous in their evening gowns, but once everything had calmed down, they would carry themselves with as much dignified femininity as a mayor's wife.

Where all the Negroes? Tycen asked, looking around with a bemused expression typical of black folk from cities with larger black populations than Knoxville.

We *are* the Negroes, I said, grabbing his hand to wend us through the gathering crowd.

While we waited for the inevitable Janet, Whitney, Shania, and Cher performances to begin, I told him about the first time I'd ever seen a drag show. I was a novice to the gay bar scene then, so green I didn't know the difference between a drag king and a drag queen.

He laughed but seemed distracted, only half-listening. Let's get a drink, he said.

The lines were too long, so I suggested we go to the bar downstairs.

We ordered Long Island iced teas, and I started back toward the stairs, but Tycen stopped me.

I wanna dance, he said.

Now? But what about the show?

Fuck the show. I want . . . to . . . dance, he said, pointing to the sunken floor, a dedicated space for entering into the center of attention if one were seeking it.

We watched a horde do just that, strutting from the perimeters when the first bars of OutKast's "I Like the Way" played on the speakers.

Tycen began a slow groove with his hips, his arms beckoning me to follow him, his hands accompanying with come-hither fingers. He sang the chorus as we pushed our way through a web of white, sweating flesh into the middle of the floor, our cups held high to prevent spillage.

What is it he's after? I wondered, not quite gauging his intentions. He guarded himself so well, but whatever he was up to resided inside his voice, in how his tongue lingered on each phrase of the song with too much emphasis, a latent desire.

And whatever it was, I already was willing . . . to do what to him, with him, exactly? Wrap my fingers around his private parts?

I had more to think about when he spun me around and began grinding his crotch against my ass. *So what is this now? What next?*

Because he was a couple inches taller than me, I simply leaned back into his body, fully dependent on him to support my weight.

His free arm tightened around my waist as he rested his warm face against my cheek.

He smelled of Burberry and faintly of liquor.

We didn't grind but swayed to the soulful rhythm, to the jazz.

But I wanted the grind, for his hands to cup the roundest parts of my body, to enter the various splits as he whispered wet into my ear, I love the way you move.

And then the song was over and fading into the next.

I started to break away, but he pulled me back.

I'm not done dancing, he said.

Oh, you're not? I said.

Nuh, uh. Not even a little.

———

I insisted on refreshing our drinks and braved a long line while Tycen swayed by himself on the dance floor.

Except when I returned with our drinks, he was no longer alone. A swarm of frenzied whiteboys were offering themselves to him, a rotation of demonstrations to alert him to their flexibility, their ample proportions and undeniable yearning. He could have one or all of them—a buyer's market.

I stood and watched, wondering what it was about blackboys that enticed whiteboys so much.

Was it Tycen's Negro lips?

His Negro nose?

His size eleven feet?

His hands, ass . . . his dick print?

Judging by his hands and feet alone, I was sure those whiteboys had put much faith in accurately calculating what Tycen was packing.

This scene reminded me so much of my trip to Key West earlier that spring. I'd gone down with some friends from work, all whiteboys, and the first night there, we went to a gay bar that actually held auctions as a way to help their patrons procure "dates," otherwise known as a guaranteed one-night stand.

My friends thought it would be funny as hell to put a blackboy on the block to see how much the whiteboys would be willing to spend.

I was curious, too, and nervous as I made my way past a throng of frat boys who expressed an excited drunkenness that finely toed the line between no-homo and bi-curiosity. I walked up the ramp to the stage, stood next to the auctioneer's podium, and waited for him to quiet the room, for him to begin the bidding at fifty dollars (*And who'll give me sixty* . . .

do I hear seventy . . .) and on up until he said, Sold for five hundred dollars to the five boys from . . .

I was now their Mandingo, their I've-never-been-with-a-black-man man, and their faces flushed with expectation, spread into grins as though they were wondering, *Is it true what they say?*

I didn't fully grasp what I'd gotten myself into, so I focused on the individual whiteboys who appeared to have come alone and stood in the back with their hands tented over their bulging crotches, paralyzed by their own beautiful reticence. These boys, I presumed, were intrigued by the prospect of the auction but were too afraid to partake in it; they were the type to dance with lesbians because it was safe, to hide in shadows so they wouldn't be seen wetting their lips when they spied the pockets of men gyrating against another, wrapped in indigo glow. They were deep-in-the-closet boys who couldn't use frat-boys-gone-wild behavior as an alibi for their presence here.

They hated songs like Britney Spears's "Toxic" or loved them only in private.

They wanted to know what carried on behind those curtains, in those rooms further cordoned off with velvet rope, but they would not dare to venture too far away from the nearest exit signs.

These were the boys I liked best, who weren't so eager in public, preferring instead to ravish you as soon as they were certain no one else was looking.

I was sure some of them who were too afraid to put in a bid would go home, lie in bed, and tremble from one hand's manual labor, perhaps imagining all the blackboys they'd like to see heaved up on a block like the one that held me.

Or perhaps if they were drunk enough and horny enough, they would accept an offer for sex, but only with a man bearing their likeness, a man who also needed to retain absolute anonymity, which could also mean that instead of being ravished by an insatiable libido, sex might end with no alarms or bells, no cigarettes or abandoned whiskey glasses on the windowsill, no stale, funky odor lingering in the room because who would provide the passion?

When it was over, I could imagine one of them grabbing the articles of clothing he left in a single heap on the floor after nervously undressing instead of collecting them from various places: the back of a chair or one of the bedposts, or on the windowsill thrown atop the glass of whiskey and, for a fun story to tell later, from the ceiling fan where his draws hung.

He would leave their trysting place with his head bowed. The same way I did when I was finally led down the plank by the arms, the torso, following behind those whiteboys whose faces were still stamped with insidious grins as we made our way behind a curtain, toward a room marked off with velvet ropes.

———

It took a month after our excursion to the Carousel—and several more visits to my apartment sans Perry—before Tycen and I began *sleeping* together. Not having sex, per se, since he wanted to fuck me, but after LeShaun, I vowed never to be fucked again.

We spent our time together usually at my apartment. Often on the couch watching TV with our hands inside each other's underwear.

He'd talk to his friends on the phone, referring to me as his boyfriend, though I wasn't sure if his friends understood if Tycen meant Perry or me.

He liked to stick his finger in my nose because he knew how much I hated it, but it tickled him. He saw it as a sign that we were close. Performing gross acts was apparently one of the purest forms of intimacy.

My displays of affection included buying Tycen a tan, suede winter coat from Wilson's—even though it was the height of August—which I tried on in the store and found a touch too roomy, but on Tycen's more muscular frame, I knew it would fit perfectly.

I called him over one afternoon while Perry was at work so I could model the coat for him. I decided to wear nothing else except a pair of underwear I turned into a makeshift thong.

I waited for him to knock on the door so I could position myself at the entrance. I wanted him to practically slam into me when I told him to come in.

He had the same idea as I did, asking me to turn as he felt the fabric.

This is fire, he said almost absently.

My legs, you mean? I said, pulling up the hem of the coat to the top of my bare thigh.

Oh, I'll get to that later, he said. But first I need you to walk for me.

I strutted the hallway to the front door and back as he looked on quietly. I toyed with him, spinning with the coat open to show him I was seminude underneath, venturing close but never close enough to be touched, though he tried, succeeding only in swiping at the air.

He intended this to be a game as much as I did, so I rewarded him with a peck on the mouth and repeated my strut up and down the hallway.

Sensing when I was readying for an about-face, he leaned forward off the door, where he'd been posting, to kiss me deeper, using his teeth gently to cling to my bottom lip.

I quickly pulled away and sashayed to the other end of the hallway, near my bedroom. And when I turned around, Tycen was slowly removing his clothes.

I leaned, framed in the bedroom doorway, admiring him.

How he placed his shoes beside the door, rolled his socks into a ball, and stuffed them inside his shoes.

How he peeled off his jeans, folded them across the living room chair.

How he yanked his shirt over his head, folded it longwise, and laid it across the jeans.

He walked toward me wearing only his underwear.

He waited until he was inside the bedroom to pull his boxer briefs past his ass, to wiggle them down his legs.

When he stepped out of them, he summoned me with his finger.

I started to remove the suede coat, but he said, No, baby, leave it on.

He pushed me back onto the bed, his erection poking me just above my navel.

He crawled between my legs, pressing against my chest to lay me flat.

He kissed my neck, tongue tickling my earlobes, then my chest, pinching my nipples in his teeth, then all the way to my toes, lifting my legs to kiss underneath my thighs, which he then, in a sudden move, propped on his shoulders.

He reached down to the waistband of my underwear, pulled the makeshift thong from between my ass and up my calves until they cleared my feet, and tossed them over his head.

I was nervous, expecting him to try to penetrate me. But he didn't. He slid himself between the thickest part of my thighs, bearing his weight upon me as he bent my knees closer to my chest. I felt my tailbone rise as he maneuvered himself between my legs, panting until I heard a hoarse whisper— *oh, fuck . . . goddamn*—and felt him come, feeling along my splattered torso while he knelt in front of me catching his breath. And when he did, he collapsed on top of me, using his chest to smear his semen across my skin. I'm rubbing myself in, he said. Yet I felt sticky, unclean, feckless, and irredeemable, and I wanted to wash up.

But still, and I wouldn't know it then, this would be the happiest I'd be with a man for many years. It would be in this very moment, Tycen nuzzling my neck and me still wearing the winter coat, both of our legs intertwined, never minding the heat that caused my skin to become slick as if a thin sheet of sweat were being drawn over me. This felt every bit of what I'd imagined a real relationship would be like.

In the darkness, I lay wondering if Tycen and I had reached a fork in the road. I had ruined my relationship with Perry, except he didn't know it yet. I asked Tycen about his relationship with Perry, considering how much time the two of us had been spending together. He wouldn't respond right away, and I didn't really want to hear his answer. I was simply thinking out loud, and I regretted it immediately. So I got him erect again and slipped him between my thighs like before, let him play with my *button*, as he liked to call it, because I was convinced he could charm me into going all the way someday, and why not tease him now with what might be in store later? What fun would it be to discover what he was willing to do to hit this?

———

Tycen didn't spend the night. He went home to Perry and took the coat with him. I asked him how he was going to explain it.

I'll tell him you gave it to me because you said it didn't fit, he said.

Okay, I said, so easily satisfied with his answer, so gullible to think Perry would accept that reason without suspicion.

You look worried, he said.

Not really, I said with a shrug, lying.

Let's go to Atlanta for Pride next month, he said, changing the subject.

What about Perry? How you . . .

Let me worry about Perry. You wanna go or not?

Mmm hmm.

Good. Now smack me one, I gotta get home.

We lingered in that kiss, neither of us aware of what the fates had in store for us.

———

Yes, we went to Atlanta for Pride the next month, September.

The first night there, we wandered Piedmont Park, the epicenter of events, but spent most of the time with a group of blackboys who were performing Prancing J-sette routines and catwalking. One modelesque twink commandeered a majority of the adulation dished out that evening with his expert walk down the runway: shoulders back and down, chin forward, body slightly leaned back in an elongated line, his feet strutting forward somewhat crossed, which gave his hips a magnificent wiggle. He was quite spectacular. I didn't expect to see him ever again once I left Tycen at the park—I'll only be gone for a little bit, I told him—to catch up with my best friend, Jerome, whom I hadn't seen since I transferred from Tennessee State two years earlier.

But when I returned to the room after Jerome dropped me off, I found Tycen on the bed with that runway twink between his legs, dry humping.

I left immediately, hearing Tycen's voice calling after me, and rushed off into the night, crying as I stumbled from one overpass to another, thankful for the number of streetlights that prevented me from drifting around completely in the dark.

The streets weren't as filthy as I would've expected them to be, so I sat on the slope of an overpass several blocks from the hotel, contemplating whether I could sleep beneath it.

But of course I couldn't.

After a while, I walked back to the hotel. It was after four in the morning, and I sat in the lobby, not ready to go back to the room.

I contemplated an absurd combination of fear (would Tycen still be in bed with him?), anger (that Tycen was in bed with him in the first place), and jealousy and shame (that Tycen wasn't committed to me).

The night auditor approached me after a few minutes to tell me that a young man had been looking for me a couple hours before.

I thanked him even though I wasn't sure why or how he knew I was the one Tycen had been looking for.

When I carefully opened the door of our room to peer inside, I heard Tycen's light snoring. It was dark, and I could barely make out the shape of his body hunched on its side.

I didn't want to share a bed with him, so I took a couple of pillows from what should have been my side of the bed and headed to the bathroom.

I pulled two large towels from the towel rack and wrapped them around me as I lay down on the hard, cold tile floor, hoping they would provide me both warmth and cushioning.

I worried about having to ride back to Tennessee with Tycen later that afternoon.

This was certainly the end of us.

And just wait until Perry finds out, I thought.

But until we'd gone to Atlanta, Tycen and I were two cheaters pretending to be a couple. Two weeks before, we were standing at my door the way cheaters do, planning a trip together, when in reality, we were preparing best practices for how to bamboozle an unsuspecting victim. We sucked each other's tongues nearly out of the other's mouth. So brazen and ravenous and thoughtless we were, both of us entering deeper into that place where danger awaited us. And Tycen left for his and Perry's apartment with our plans for Atlanta secured, where I imagined he slipped into bed with my best friend and told him lies about his day. And Perry probably lapped them up like cool water. They'd likely cuddled beneath a blanket to watch TV, or maybe they'd fucked and soiled the sheets with their sweat. I was alone in my own bed, contemplating these very thoughts. And after a while, each of us finally closed our eyes, and no one—not yet—needed to worry about confronting what slept right there beside him.

You Don't Have to Like It

'd been experiencing several nights of little sleep, nights I'd spent positioning myself so I no longer felt this drowning sensation in my chest, positions that found me, ultimately, placing a pillow against the living room wall so that I might finally fall asleep standing straight up, which I decided was unusual. And so I called Mama, as I'd done only a couple of months before, to return me to St. Mary's Hospital so that I might know what was happening inside my body.

An EKG and an hour or so later, the urgent care cardiologist explained that because he discovered my heart was functioning at only 23 percent, this indicated congestive heart failure or, more importantly, he emphasized, a severe chance of sudden cardiac arrest. I was admitted into the hospital at once.

In the days that followed, in addition to my parents' bedside vigilance and check-ins from nurses, techs, and administrative staff members, several doctors had been consulting one another, rummaging through their expert knowledge until they arrived at a consensus as to why a man thirty-six years old had congestive heart failure but no family history of heart disease. They noted in my chart, *possible causes of systolic heart failure for this patient: reports history of cocaine use and also reports history of extensive alcoholism.*

I'd been having trouble maneuvering my arms and hands behind me to cinch together the back of my hospital gown as tightly as I could to keep the cold air off my skin. The effort took the breath from me, the result, surely, of my heart condition.

I wondered if the seams of the windows had come unglued somehow, allowing in a steady stream of cold air that would turn everything to frost. I bunched myself against the pillows and tugged the blanket and sheets close to my chest to keep from trembling. I humored myself by imagining that if the urban legend were true, then my shivering was due to someone—at that very moment—walking across the future site of my grave.

Dr. Flowers was the attending physician, and on the third day of my stay in the hospital, he informed me of the possible etiologies for congestive heart failure—in other words, how this could have happened to me.

It's possible, he said, that extensive alcoholism damaged your heart to the point that now it's failing.

What I heard was, *Why do you drink so much?* But I didn't hear that in Dr. Flowers's imagined voice. It was Mama's, from a night back in 2002, when I was twenty-two. She sat at a dining room table watching Daddy and me drink—shots and chasers well into evening, until finally she got up from the table and never returned.

I'd gotten so drunk, I only noticed she'd disappeared when I noticed she was no longer shaking her head at the two of us.

I found her in her bedroom. She said nothing initially when I asked what she was doing in there alone. She looked at me, blinking back tears, and asked, Why do you drink so much?

Her face was so long with heartache. I tried to locate where I'd seen that look before. Not since her own daddy had died suddenly many years ago had I seen her this way. She so seldom cried, and now her tears encouraged me to turn the entire night into an operetta. Perhaps because I felt protected by an armor of drunkenness, I decided on that day, in that moment, I would come out to her. I always felt that delivering the news to her would be much easier than telling Daddy. She had always been the go-to parent, but her tears caught me off guard.

Was she the same woman who, when we lived in Lonsdale, would toss the football with my younger brother and me in the yard and do the girly things with my sister?

The same woman who fed us foods she knew we would want to eat rather than whatever she felt like cooking?

Each night, she ironed our school clothes and laid them out and checked on us on her way to work so early in the morning while we still slept.

Daddy, by comparison, was a military soldier and ordered absolute compliance from his children. This meant bedtime at eight, and in the mornings, he'd wake us by simulating an army drill, flicking the light switch on and off with one hand while using the other to beat against the bedroom wall.

He disallowed talking at the dinner table, and we were dismissed only when we cleaned our plates.

He would smack my brother and me upside the head for minor household infractions, or he would take a leather belt to our bare asses for more flagrant ones, like the time a convenience store clerk caught me stealing bubble gum and called home to report me.

So even though I didn't know why I drank so much, in response to Mama's question, I told her I drank so much because I was gay. In fact, I didn't think I drank that much at all. And it certainly wasn't because I was gay.

Mama seemed at first to have nothing more to say on the matter, and then there was so much she needed to unburden.

I always knew, she said. I didn't want to believe it, but something told me.

Daddy, soon after, joined us in the room, asking, What's wrong, why is she crying? I'd always feared coming out to my daddy, so here was the real test, and without a beat, I blurted out to him: Because I told Mama I'm gay.

Surprisingly, he took hold of me in his arms and cradled my head against his shoulder.

It's okay, he said. We'll keep this in the family.

My younger brother, who was twenty at the time, whom no one had noticed in the doorway, stood mute, a reluctant witness to our huddle.

He stomped away, and I followed him outside into the humid-hot air of August. He wasted no time, not even bothering to turn and face me, invoking God and the Bible and the sin of homosexuality—how God didn't approve of or didn't like it or that he had instructed us to do only God knows what.

I wanted to choke my brother and to wrest his God from the night sky. Under the streetlamps, I gnashed my teeth, clenched my jaw, forcing him to look me in the eye until he pointed his finger at me: Don't fucking grit your teeth at me, Darius.

I sulked away, wishing my baby sister had been there so I'd have an ally. Not Daddy's *let's keep it in the family* but someone in the family who would have called bullshit on that bullshit.

I returned to the house, crying. I wanted to go the fuck home, back to my apartment where I could be alone.

Daddy intercepted me at the door.

No, you're staying here tonight, he said. I'll fix us all breakfast in the morning.

So I stayed the night, and the next morning, we ate the breakfast Daddy had promised—eggs, biscuits, sausage, bacon, several glasses of orange juice I quietly spiked with vodka.

———

Dr. Flowers had more news. My heart condition had other possible causes.

Several months after coming out to Mama, I decided to tell her while we were shopping at the grocery store on a Sunday afternoon that I'd exposed myself to HIV. We'd started in the produce section looking for fruit. She sampled a handful of grapes, then inspected a variety of apples but decided against them. She placed a bunch of bananas in her cart and wheeled over to the cantaloupe and honeydew but became distracted by the watermelon. She didn't thump or smell them like one was supposed to do but slightly rolled each one back and forth, looking at me as if I might help her decide which one was the best.

You still eat watermelon, don't you? she asked, hovering over a large one as if she were wielding her carving knife, waiting for me to give her the go-ahead to slice into the melon's red meat.

I wanted to tell her no, that I hated it. Admit to her that even as a kid I hadn't liked watermelon or being made to sit on the front porch of our first house on East Fifth Avenue in the warm spring sunshine to eat it, to let the juice run down my chin, spitting out the seeds, tossing the rind across the street like a one-way boomerang.

I shook my head no, then told her that I had recently gotten tested for HIV. I walked our cart away from the produce, failing to mention that I'd had to get tested because I'd been hooking up with Tycen who, I learned from Perry, turned out to be positive.

She was silent, walking ahead of me, her composure noticeably shifting from cheerful to troubled.

But don't worry, I said. I'm negative.

You see, this is what I'm talking about, she said, as though I'd ruined a perfectly fine day grocery shopping.

What is that supposed to mean? I asked.

Nothing, Darius, she said.

I hesitated to press her further. I'd just told her that her gay son had been exposed to HIV because he'd been intimate with a man who tested positive for the virus.

And what had she told me when I'd come out to her those months ago? That she knew I was gay or at least that she had suspected I was for years. And hadn't she implied that her mother's intuition was infallible? Hadn't she meant to warn me how concerned she was for me and this lifestyle? Had she not said she didn't want to believe I was gay? It would worry her endlessly. She was my mother and couldn't help but want to protect me from those consequences that frightened her most. That I had sex with men. Only, she couldn't say it.

What's wrong, Mama? I asked.

She continued to push her cart down the aisle, selecting an assortment of canned vegetables, thinking how to respond to me. I'd seen this careful deliberation many times before, when I was a young boy and she had to decide between disappointing me or doing what was best for me. This was probably why she was so matter of fact when she finally said, You don't have to like it, Darius.

She delivered her words as if they were borne from instinct: *You don't have to like it.* She responded to my question, *What's wrong?* with an answer that was intentionally shorthand, encompassing everything that *it* must represent to her: desire, fear, recklessness, homosex.

My initial impulse was to forget what she'd said so her words wouldn't erase my fondest versions of her. There came the sudden flash of me as a young boy, waiting on the corner for her to step off the K-Trans city bus in Knoxville. I'd been away for a week at summer camp, and when I returned home, she was still at work until sometime after three o'clock, when I walked to the corner to wait for her. When she stepped off the bus and saw me, she ran across the street, set down her nursing bag, and lifted me into the air to hug me. We walked back to our apartment as I talked excitedly about canoeing and venturing to the edge of a waterfall, where it was shallow enough to get out of the boat and stand over the small cliff to watch the water topple into the whirling waters below.

This was the earliest memory I had of clearly knowing how much my mother loved me. Now, a dark curtain had fallen, cordoning that memory off, and an eerie scene began to develop in which we were somehow cast into a tragedy right there in the middle of the grocery store aisle. I imagined a ghostly chorus emerging from behind the cereal boxes, the loaves of bread, gliding toward us on their shopping carts, their mouths so rife with molasses and heavy jams they could only moan deeply, expressing my grief in mournful song.

───────

We ran several tests, Dr. Flowers said. But what he didn't say was: *The results are not what we expected.*

He explained how they figured it all out, rattling off the context clues for what could have caused congestive heart failure: extensive alcohol abuse; other factors, such as a few recent bouts of pneumonia I'd overcome; my sexual history.

My sexual history? Is this what put me in the hospital? Was it so obvious that my sex life was indeed the culprit, as evidenced by the assemblage of papers bulging inside the file folder Dr. Flowers held in his hands, as if there were pages of salacious stories threatening to scatter onto the floor, dispersing so that each sheet would collide noisily, all that rowdy shuffling reminiscent of the muffled noises of the many men who filled many rooms during many encounters from many years ago?

Your heart condition could've been caused by a virus, Dr. Flowers said. So we checked.

Of course, I perked up when I heard that word *virus.* How often he repeated it in what seemed to be a series of fragmented phrases: You may have contracted a *virus*; we cannot rule out the possibility that your heart failure is due to a *virus* we discovered; Mr. *virus, virus, virus . . .*

Somehow, I missed Dr. Flowers clearly asking me, Are you aware that you're HIV positive?

———

I couldn't pinpoint when it was exactly, but I used to experience these inklings that something was *wrong*, had always been *wrong*, with my body.

That's why I wasn't too surprised, really, when Dr. Flowers said my tests had come back positive for HIV. I might have flinched at the news, the way you do when looking away from the needle that pricks your skin to draw blood. You don't have to see it to feel it.

I'd just been told that I'd contracted HIV, and—as if it was my only recourse—I smirked at the news, knowing I'd squandered every opportunity I might have had to prevent this diagnosis. I chuckled so quietly that it didn't register until I felt the subtle laughter vibrating inside my chest.

How mercilessly I'd forced my body to refuse its own pleas for help.

Years I'd spent destroying my body. And when I really thought about the condition I was in—congestive heart failure, HIV—I didn't know how much more of this I could continue to find so laughable, so absurd.

I thought about the diminishing pleasures of succumbing to lust.

I thought about death since I'd been hit with a twofer: CHF and HIV.

I thought about people's capacity for empathy.

I thought about petty grievances, of being talked about behind my back, how people would worry themselves, knowing that even when they understood we weren't living in the 1980s heyday of the virus, they still would think of me and fear how closely they might have come to being infected themselves whenever they remembered those seemingly innocuous intimacies, like the one time we pecked on the mouth in greeting or gave one another lingering hugs at our departure just to feel the warmth of the other's skin a little longer.

It was ruthless, the way those notions overwhelmed my consciousness.

I was filled with so much regret, my life reduced to a list of *ifs*:

if I had not drunk so much and snorted so much and tripped so much and spent so many nights begging for attention like a castaway beneath the highway underpasses, a beggar rejected to the gutters;

if I had not smiled deceitfully into all those blank yet still bereaved faces of my friends who saw me as a man turning slowly into a disease;

if sex had not been too easy to find nor had continued to be always a solution;

if sex would never have to begin with me pleading for a man not to be afraid of my body;

if only I could start all over again, an innocent boy swooning outside the fence of a basketball court, enjoying a spear of summer grass set between his teeth.

———

When I was able, I looked Dr. Flowers in the face, into the perfect candor in his eyes, and told him that I hadn't been aware that I had HIV. He appeared sincerely compassionate, the way only a man who probably gardened on weekends, spending hours with his hands plunging through soft dirt, could contain such grace.

As he turned to leave, as if I'd gotten myself into some kind of trouble, I said to him, You aren't going to tell my parents, are you?

He looked at me, surprised. Not unless you'd like me to.

No, I said.

———

When Mama and Daddy returned to my hospital room, it was strange to see them together. They'd been divorced for close to a decade, but as long as Daddy hadn't had too much to drink—he was prone to gestures of apology and reconciliation when he was drunk—Mama would tolerate him.

I would like to have kept the news of my HIV status from them, to relish the way they took turns ensuring that I was comfortable enough, that I'd had enough to eat, before moving on to more general topics of conversation, as if all there was to worry over was the condition of my heart.

They lacked that fearful trembling in their voices that reverberated in my own when I asked Dr. Flowers if he planned to tell them the test results. But even if I lied by omission, keeping this news from them was a lie nonetheless that I couldn't bear to commit. So I told them.

Afterward, the quiet room.

Mama retreated to the bathroom.

Daddy sat in a chair, nodding his head, chewing on his lower lip. Okay. Okay. We'll deal with this as a family, he said. This is our business. Nobody needs to know about our business.

Clarence . . . just be quiet, Mama said, though we could barely hear her.

I got out of bed and made my way to her. She stood before the bathroom mirror with the lights off. I suppose she needed a place to grieve with some degree of privacy. A shadow in which she could hide. She could have closed the door, but that would have shut me out. Very faintly, I could see where tears had left streaks on her face, and we were once again at that familiar juncture, my mother—who so seldom cried—made into a woman who could no longer refuse to.

You don't have to like it, she'd said after learning that there was only one man who had exposed me to this virus and that it had worried her. But things were different now. I'd slept with enough men to colonize my body. Each time I experienced a tickle in my throat or sensed the encroachment of fever, it may have been from a small city being constructed within me by a virus.

Whenever she cried for me, perhaps she cried for having always known the consequences I might face as her gay son; perhaps she cried from knowing there was so much a mother couldn't do to protect her child; perhaps she felt a failure on her part but also an understanding that she wasn't at fault; and so perhaps she cried for having to accept that her role as my mother was a constant negotiation between wanting to do something and having the ability to do so.

I'm sure she knew this. Of course she did, just as she did one night long ago in my childhood, when our family still lived in Lonsdale, and Daddy, my brother, and sister were out somewhere else—I don't remember where. So Mama and I stayed up late in the living room, dancing together in our socks, not slowly but with lots of rhythmic movement that extended beyond the proximity of our bodies. The lamp was lit, dousing us in dim light, which was probably why I didn't see the television set when I flung myself wildly across the room and felt myself sliding toward the TV stand. And then the crash.

Glass shattered everywhere.

I was afraid immediately of the repercussions, but Mama simply moved me out of the way of the shards and went for a broom to sweep up the broken pieces until she was sure she'd gotten all that she could see. She said I needed shoes, so I ran upstairs to grab the first pair I saw and slipped them on, while downstairs, the volume on the stereo grew louder than it was before. I bounded back down, halting at the bottom step to find Mama had continued dancing without me, her body dipping and swaying, her neck swiveling to the melody, her fingers snapping to accentuate the beat, and so I left her alone to enjoy herself, and I listened for the song I knew she hummed in her throat.

Skin Hunger

Touch me, touch the palm of your hand to my body as I pass,
Be not afraid of my body.

—Walt Whitman

A few days after my release from St. Mary's Hospital, my brother called to ask if I'd heard the news about my best friend, Jerome.

No, I said.

He died, man, my brother said.

My first thought was how did my brother know this before I did? My second was, how did he die?

I asked my brother.

I don't know, he said. I thought you would be able to find that out.

I thanked my brother. Said goodbye.

Eventually, I would find out that Jerome's HIV had advanced to full-blown AIDS, and on one of the days that I was lying in a hospital bed, perhaps turning the pillow over to its cooler side so I could rest more comfortably, or perhaps while checking Facebook for all the well-wishes posted on my page, Jerome had died alone in his apartment in Chicago.

———

It'd been nearly four years since Jerome and I had last seen each other during Tennessee State University's centennial homecoming. We spent the weekend festivities catching up, and before I departed back home to Knoxville, he asked me to consider moving to San Diego, where he lived.

Uproot yourself, he said. Just think about it and call me when you make up your mind.

I never made the call, and I didn't know when I might've until I was diagnosed with HIV myself. As soon as I was released to go home, I knew I needed to call him. I even *prepared* myself to contend with his possible shock and preconceptions, all the things he might've said—*I thought you was a top, boy! Whose nut you done caught!*

His reassuring platitudes—*Well, at least it's not a death sentence anymore. We can survive it.*

But Jerome was too incalculable to ever predict what he may or may not have said.

In our decades-long friendship, our shared seropositive status would have only strengthened our bond.

But he was gone. And I had to channel his strength somehow for the long road ahead.

————

The medical social worker at St. Mary's told me to expect a call from the Centers of Excellence at the Knox County Health Department. And as if on cue, in the midst of my grieving Jerome's death, a volunteer called. His name was Ray—he didn't give a last name. He was very matter-of-fact.

It's urgent business, he told me, that you've tested positive for HIV.

Yes, I know, I said.

So you do confirm this diagnosis, he said.

I was confused that he didn't seem to understand this was what I meant. I wondered about his age. I could tell he was old. His voice labored with a raspy drawl that decades of use had worn thin. But this was a petty thought, indicating my grief, I supposed. Though a part of me, because of his age, felt judged by a man who sounded generations removed from me, a man who I assumed might not approve of my lifestyle, to say nothing of what my lifestyle had caused.

Yes, I confirm, I said.

Please provide me the known names and numbers of your needle-sharing or sexual partners, he said.

Needle-sharing?

Yes, needle-sharing and sexual partners.

I don't do drugs . . . anymore, I said, neglecting to clarify that my drug use never included syringes. I would fixate on this oversight for days afterward, worried that Ray would assume I was once some kind of junkie.

Well, your sexual partners, then. Names and numbers, please.

I didn't have the names and numbers to help Ray with his contact tracing. He would call at least twice more, each time more irritated than the last that I hadn't come up with these names and numbers. You do know how serious this is, don't you? People deserve to know that their lives might be at stake, he'd said, making it clear that I harbored a contagion and could have possibly spread it. I was a public health crisis.

Perhaps my reaction to Ray's phone calls was a manifestation of some form of vanity. I was known for staring into a mirror after a fresh haircut, examining the clean, razor-sharp lines, which rewarded my face with depth, and how my mustache and goatee were perfectly yoked, how they framed my mouth, made it supple. Now I feared no man would want me, might not ever answer my desire to be touched and his desire to be touched back by me, physically, spiritually, emotionally. The grim facts of my past remained: I engaged in too much touching without regard to my health. Too much democratizing the body until I found myself infected with HIV and a persistent, awful notion haunting my thoughts: how often would I have to plead with a man not to be afraid of my body?

———

Six months after my HIV diagnosis, in mid-June of 2016, after faithfully taking daily doses of Complera, then Odefsy, my viral load measured fewer than fifty copies of the virus per milliliter of blood, which meant I was undetectable.

Except I didn't know what this meant, exactly. I'd seen advertisements that Undetectable = Untransmittable, or U = U. Initially, I experienced a feeling of disbelief not unlike my reaction to learning I was HIV positive. The doctor made it plain that the virus could not be detected. My body wasn't only healthy but there was virtually no risk of transmitting the virus to others. It was easy to misinterpret this news as an occasion to celebrate being *cured*. I nearly did. And the doctor made sure to clarify this. Nevertheless, once I fully adapted to the gravity of learning my HIV was undetectable, I felt an overwhelming sense of renewal, where nothing seemed familiar to me, as if I were experiencing life all over again.

Arriving home after the doctor's appointment, still high on the news, I stood at the window overlooking the backyard, staring at the horizon, at the trees breathing on the mountaintop off in the distance. My limbs felt slack, a sensation I hadn't felt since I'd moved from my mama's house into a place of my own, exhilarated as I turned the key in my new keyhole that opened my new door into a house so desperately empty yet utterly pristine with its white walls, the lingering aroma of lemon-scented Pine Sol, and the gloss of linoleum scrubbed clean, each cranny like a dried-out ravine. I became almost devastated to the point of a nervous breakdown, as if somehow I could lose it all, in an instant, the beauty of the well-kept oak cabinetry, the fluorescent glow inside the ceiling's frosted globe light fixtures, three bedrooms, any one of them I could choose to belong only to me, but especially the windows so abundant all I could anticipate was the possibility of so much natural light rousing me as I wandered each room until the day peeled away like a scab, until what was left was the vibrant wound of night with its stars and moon and haze of mountaintops pulsing with all those breathing trees in the distance that surely, come each evening, I would be beholden to, twisting open the vertical blinds to lean in so close to the pane my breath would appear parceled against the glass as if the last breath I'd ever take, this breath condensing like tears on the glass, like dew falling from tree leaves to the grass I'd feel slick against the soles of my bare feet whenever I stepped outdoors, marveled by a kernel of want that had been fleshed out into a full-bloomed desire to live in this house forever. Like this body I now felt I could live in for an eternity.

———

I wanted companionship again, so I dipped first back into the dating app pool of Plenty of Fish, then cast my net wider to OKCupid, Tinder, and, perhaps mischievously, Grindr.

I composed similar profiles on each platform with unfiltered pictures to make me appear closer to my actual age, relying on my skincare regiments of facial peels, lotions, serums, Noxzema, and the like to make myself naturally attractive, desirable. Again, my reliance on vanity proved critical to my survival in this new world of the seroconverted and those who were not.

In my profile, I claimed to be a sapiophile— a man attracted to intelligence—a pretension masquerading as charm. I ticked off other random traits to inform anyone interested that I was a published writer with a master's degree; gregarious; possibly interested; open to suggestions; a foodie; a baker; a sometime cinephile, especially *Call Me by*

Your Name; a fan always of the Cartoon Network; *SpongeBob SquarePants*; *Forensic Files*; *Golden Girls*; HGTV; *Fixer Upper*, Jeff Devlin; the Property Brothers; celebrity crushes: Chance the Rapper; Frank Ocean; celebrity *art-throb*: Timothée Chalamet; proudly sober; sullenly single; a night owl; a hostile homebody; favorite color blue; a dog lover; prefer over thirty and under fifty; HIV positive; undetectable; compatible with Sagittarius?; moon in Pisces.

————

I disclosed I was HIV positive but undetectable because it allowed me to be transparent, but also, quite frankly, I wanted to present myself as a safe choice. A man would know who he was getting with me. And even for the men using these apps, I had faith in their capacity for empathy.

But I began to have my doubts after reading several online articles about other HIV positive men—also undetectable—and their dating experiences. Responding to these articles, I was both horrified and enraged by the number of white gay men who made it plain in the comments section that the stigma of being HIV positive—particularly for black gay men and other gay men of color—was alive and well:

Stop trying to normalize HIV . . .

I think a lot of these poz men create this problem for themselves in the community . . .

I understand what undetectable means, I'm not dumb, I'm just not going to believe some random guy off Grindr when he says he takes his pills every day . . .

No person with a sane conscience wants to risk infection . . .

You can't shame others for not wanting to touch you with a fifty-foot pole . . .

If you got HIV by carelessly sleeping around, then you've only yourself to blame . . .

You are not owed a relationship . . .

You are not owed sex . . .

You are not owed attention . . .

You are not owed someone's affections . . .

———

As quickly as I'd joined (or rejoined) those dating apps, I just as quickly stopped using them.

I told myself I was better off alone. At least for the time being.

Or I did the thing I said I wouldn't do: wallow in the past, regretful for not emboldening myself to make my feelings known to men whom, had I been braver, or at least more adventurous, may have been *the one*, as if this would have made me less inclined to engage in risky sexual behaviors with multiple partners, as if this would have saved me. *What if . . .*

I thought especially about a whiteboy named Lucas, even though I, at my most generous, had begun to give serious side-eye to gay whiteboys for being the terrorists that some of their reactions to HIV-positive individuals made them seem so bent on becoming. I thought about Lucas in spite of my want for a blackboy who wouldn't be like the many blackboys from my past who'd insisted that yes, we could rendezvous, but on the low, and that they would never consider a relationship other than a clandestine quid pro quo wherein they were absolutely going to end each and every nightly tryst spent and satisfied; meanwhile, all I could do was agree to the contract we'd entered into and hope that whatever pleasure I might derive would last long enough for me to at least take off my socks.

I thought of Lucas because I'd been suffering seriously from skin hunger, from the type of touch deprivation that, for sex positive individuals like me, felt agonizing for the sheer fact that I was also HIV positive. So, yes, when I remembered Lucas—the blue-eyed ginger with gorgeous teeth and the smile to prove it—I remembered how thrilling it was to play that guessing game of *what if* that first started when he and I had worked together at Chesapeake's—he as a dishwasher, and I, a bartender.

Lucas was slick thin, Boho chic, and a sometime vegetarian. Unlike many back-of-the-house employees, he enjoyed hanging out after work with the front-of-the-house crew.

At our favorite bar in the Old City, ten to twelve of us would cram inside our favorite booth; he'd always end up beside me, the two of us with our shoulders and thighs squished against the other's, elbow to elbow, drinks in one hand and cigarettes in the other, their glowing embers raised high in the air to prevent cherry-bombing the other.

While the others talked shop about work, we bonded over our mutual affection for the poet Jack Gilbert. Our lives happen between the memorable, I remember saying one night. He nodded in agreement, as if the words were mine, not recognizing they were Gilbert's, from his poem "Highlights and Interstices."

———

I had my *what if. . .* moment with Lucas one night when he and I went out after work, just the two of us, to one of the busier bars in Market Square, only a few blocks from our job. It was quite loud, making it difficult for either of us to understand the other. We mostly yelled in each other's ears.

And then he said suddenly, out of context of the conversation we'd been trying to have, I've never kissed

a man. But if I had to choose one to kiss, I would choose
you . . . but I'm straight.

Or maybe this was precisely the conversation he was
trying to have, the point he'd been trying to make to me
all along, only the message had been subsumed by the noise,
or it'd gotten garbled so that his words entered my ear out
of sequence. And so what I heard first was the last thing he
said—*But I'm straight*—which would have made me wonder
how this non sequitur had come to pass. Though it's just as
likely that I was being deliberately dense, that I'd heard him
just fine and had become excitable at the notion of us kissing,
and so I scoffed, bitter, and never acknowledged that what
he'd implied was that he found me desirable. And his saying
but I'm straight was merely an opportunity for me to seduce
him, which, perhaps was what he'd wanted me to do, to coax
him into intimacy, and his mentioning he was straight was
simply code for: *so whatever happens between us needs to stay
between us.*

No one needs to know.

And no strings attached.

I remember he smiled at me. Then he laughed and
slapped my thigh, leaned in the way a man does when he
is unashamed to invite the other to touch, to slake a thirst.
Lucas's beer sloshed inside the pint glass, and a little spilled
over the rim.

And then he looked at me so earnestly and said, I just thought you should know.

I didn't know how to respond, so I took the opportunity to remove a stray hair I'd noticed earlier on his shirt. I thought to myself that I could save it in my wallet and gather others until I had his whole oily head in there.

Only now does it seem obvious what Lucas had been trying to tell me that night. But I didn't press him. I couldn't. I'd already devolved into that old cliché where the gay boy falls for the straight boy—hence the reason I imagined a collection of his hair in my wallet—and the buck had to stop there, which meant that the strange manifestations of our desires—Lucas with his, me with mine—would be forever consigned to the land of shoulda, coulda, woulda.

Though this didn't stop me from having recurring dreams that the origin story of our relationship was some queer variation of the glass slipper motif in Cinderella.

All day, I'd find long, red hairs in the washing machine, coiled around the oven knobs, in the mustard of my sausages and kraut. . . . I would think to whom they might belong—someone I'd loved (or obsessed over, confusing it for love), or someone I'd just known casually, someone I'd met at a party, gazing over a keg, or perhaps someone I'd carried on a brief conversation with in an aisle at the grocery store or right before the lights dimmed to signal the start of a movie at the theater. I needed to know, so I searched through photo albums, piled them on the floor, one after the other, holding the strands against red-cropped heads, using the magnifying glass for closer comparison, but no luck. I opened the phone book, dialed numbers, names A–Z—described the hairs, entangled them, described the helixes, the knots and shadows, how each strand thickened and thinned like a snake's tail only in the softest light. Who had hair like that? No one knew. I was in fits of frustration as I sorted through piles and piles of hats in men's clothing stores, attaching strands inside the brim, picturing how his hair might flow from there like a shadow against his forehead. I'd run to the store manager, panting and sweating with bloodshot eyes, and ask for names, for clues, but I'd receive only a blank stare in return, as if I'd fabricated the whole thing—as if there was a chance the hairs were merely the light catching a scratch in the washing machine, on the oven. I'd leave the shop lion-muscled, but not of heart, for grief pitched stones against my heart as if it were an abandoned house. I'd return home, to the sites of the hairs, but they would be gone, and I couldn't help but feel like a man who'd lost his lover after a long illness and now must endure life's uninterrupted goings-on, or like a man who still felt the warmth dwindling from the empty side of the bed where a lover never slept, a lover who was never even there.

_____

The poet J. D. McClatchy once asked, Is there such a thing as unrequited friendship?

There is such a thing as unrequited friendship, only, sometimes, it masquerades as love. I would never dare to tell Lucas, *I'm in love with you,* so I told him, instead, I love you, man.

I love you, too, Darius, he said. You're like a brother to me.

I love you more than my luggage. Love you like a play cousin.

Play cousin? He said, looking a little confused, because by *play,* he didn't understand I meant *pretend,* that I had to love him from a distance, make believe I didn't care that he meant the word *love* differently from me. I had to write it off, continue to mock love. Mouth *elephant juice.*

It's just something we used to say, I told him.

We were pals, almost like two guys who meet every day after work for drinks and pick kernels of popcorn from the same bowl and argue over who pays the bill until one reminds the other it's all part of a system: one hand washes the other; you scratch my back, I scratch yours. Two guys laughing together boisterously, calming themselves only long enough for one to get the other's attention when a waitress saunters by and they remark how firm and round her ass is, which ends the similarities between those two guys and Lucas and me, for he and I could never be the companions they are.

This was the metric by which I measured my relationship with him. Perhaps the complication of an unrequited friendship prevented me from acknowledging our friendship for what it was: an un(re)solved riddle. Was it possible we were more than that but neither of us could bring himself to prove it?

Every time we parted, I'd glimpse some momentary hint of longing glistening in his face, in the way he'd embrace me in his arms or pull away, almost reluctantly it seemed, and say in a low, deep voice, *Later*, his tongue lifting on each syllable, ticking against the roof of his mouth, left to linger inches from my ear.

And then we'd go our separate ways.

At home I'd undress, smell my skin thick with smoke, rounds and rounds of beer, the occasional shots. I would not bathe. I wanted to take the whole night to bed with me.

Acknowledgments

Pieces from this memoir have appeared, in different forms, in *Salamander*, the *Brooklyn Review*, *Gargoyle*, the *Appalachian Review*, *Gertrude*, *Barren Magazine*, *Fourth Genre*, the *Arkansas International*, *Aquifer: The Florida Review Online*, *storySouth*, *Brink*, and *Intimacies in Borrowed Light*.

For their material and/or moral support, I extend my most gracious gratitude to the following individuals for this book's existence:

David Wilson * Lei Wang * Sarah Viren * Inara Verzemnieks * Alonzo Vereen * T. M. Tucker * Anne Trubek * Bonnie Sunstein * Rachel Sudbeck * Susan Steinberg * Ian Shank * Hannah Seidlitz * Emmett Rensin * Katie Prout * Alexander Pines * Andre Perry * Dina Peone * Kofi Opam * DK Nnuro * Nicolás Medina Mora * Aracely Mondragon * Phoebe

Mogharei * Emily Mester * Brittany Means * Matt McGowan * Virginia Marshall * Julia Lucas * Bryn Lovitt * Kiese Laymon * Jess Kibler * Julie Kedzie * Michael Jauchen * Rebecca Isaacs * Kerry Howley * EmmaJean Holley * Cherie Hansen-Rieskamp * Amelia Gramling * Patricia Foster * Ed Folsom * Lulu Dewey * John D'Agata * Dan Cronin * Julia Conrad * Kathleen Cole * Corey Campbell * MK Brake * Brittany Borghi * Yasmin Boakye * Sarah Blake * Brittany Bettendorf * Jumi Bello * Cat Baab-Mugira * Tony Andrews * Kaveh Akbar

About the Author

Darius Stewart is a poet and writer from Knoxville, Tennessee. He is the author of the poetry collection *Intimacies in Borrowed Light* (EastOver Press, 2022). His poems and creative nonfiction have appeared in the *Arkansas International*, the *Brooklyn Review*, *Callaloo*, *Cimarron Review*, *Fourth Genre*, *Salamander*, *Verse Daily*, and others. He holds MFAs from the Michener Center for Writers and the University of Iowa's Nonfiction Writing Program. Currently, he is a Lulu Johnson Doctoral Fellow in Literary Studies at the University of Iowa.

Printed in the USA
CPSIA information can be obtained
at www.ICGtesting.com
JSHW020314131223
53671JS00003B/5